HISTORY AND MYSTERY OF

SANTA FE AND NORTHERN

NEW MEXICO

KEN HUDNALL AND SHARON HUDNALL
OMEGA PRESS
EL PASO, TEXAS

HISTORY AND MYSTERY OF SANTA FE AND NORTHERN NEW MEXICO

COPYRIGHT © 2017 KEN HUDNALL

All rights reserved. No part of the book may be reproduced or transmitted in any form or by any means, graphic, electronic, or mechanical, including photocopying, recording, taping or by any information storage or retrieval system, without the permission in writing of the author.

OMEGA PRESS

http://www.kenhudnall.com

FIRST EDITION

Printed in the United States of America

OTHER WORKS BY THE SAME AUTHOR UNDER THE NAME KEN HUDNALL FROM OMEGA PRESS

MANHATTAN CONSPIRACY SERIES
Blood on the Apple
Capitol Crimes
Angel of Death
Confrontation

THE OCCULT CONNECTION
UFOs, Secret Societies and Ancient Gods
The Hidden Race
Flying Saucers
UFOs and the Supernatural
UFOs and Secret Societies
UFOs and Ancient Gods
Evidence of Alien Contact
Intervention
Secrets of Dulce
Unidentified Flying Objects
Sensual Alien Encounters
Strange Creatures From Time and Space
Introduction to Roswell
Alien Encounters
Mysteries of Space
Battle of Los Angeles

DARKNESS
When Darkness Falls
Fear the Darkness

SPIRITS OF THE BORDER
(with Connie Wang)
The History and Mystery of El Paso Del Norte
The History and Mystery of Fort Bliss, Texas

(with Sharon Hudnall)
The History and Mystery of the Rio Grande
The History and Mystery of New Mexico
The History and Mystery of the Lone Star State
The History and Mystery of Arizona
The History and Mystery of Tombstone, AZ
The History and Mystery of Colorado
Echoes of the Past
El Paso: A City of Secrets
Tales From the Nightshift
The History and Mystery of Sin City
The History and Mystery of Concordia
The History and Mystery of ASARCO
Military Ghosts
School Spirits
Restless spirits
Railroad Ghosts
Nautical Ghosts
Haunted Hotels
Haunted Hotels in Arizona and Colorado
Ghosts of Albuquerque
The History and Mystery of Tucson

BOOK OF SECRETS
Ancient Secrets

SHADOW WARS
The Shadow Rulers
The Secret Elite

THE ESTATE SALE MURDERS
Dead Man's Diary

A Bloody Afternoon of Fun

Northwood Conspiracy

No Safe Haven: Homeland Insecurity

Where No Car Has Gone Before

Seventy Years and No Losses: The History of the Sun Bowl

How Not To Get Published

Lost Cities and Hidden Tunnels Along the Border

Vampires, Werewolves and Things That Go Bump in The Night

Border Escapades of Billy the Kid

Criminal law for the Layman

Understanding Business Law

Language of the Law

Death of Innocence: The Life and Death of Vince Foster

The Veterans' Practice Primer

PUBLISHED BY PAJA BOOKS
The Occult Connection: Unidentified Flying Objects

PUBLISHED BY PRUNE DANISH PRESS
Why Would They Say It?

DEDICATION

As with all of my endeavors, this would not be possible without the support and assistance of my lovely wife, Sharon Hudnall.

TABLE OF CONTENTS

CHAPTER ONE 11
THE LAND OF ENCHANTMENT 11
CHAPTER TWO 45
SANTA FE, NEW MEXICO 45
    THE GLOW HOUSE 49
    THE COLLEGE OF SANTA FE 50
    GRANT CORNER INN 56
    LA FONDA HOTEL 58
    LA RESIDENCIA 60
    LA POSADA DE SANTA FE 64
    SANTA FE INDIAN SCHOOL 68
    PENITENTIARY OF NEW MEXICO, STATE FE
    71
    THE OLDEST HOUSE 76
    CASA REAL HEALTH CARE CENTER 78
    THE SCHOOL OF AMERICAN RESEARCH 79
    LEGAL TENDER SALOON 85
    NIGHT SKY GALLERY 86
    ST. VINCENT HOSPITAL 87
    THREE SISTERS BOUTIQUE 88
    CAMACHO HOUSE 90
    CHURCH OF SAN MIGUEL POR BARRIO
    ANALCO 91
    THE DEVIL HOUSE 94
    LUGUNA PUEBLO MISSION 95
    PERA BUILDING 96
    VILLAGRA BUILDING 98
CHAPTER THREE 101
TAOS, NEW MEXICO 101
    GOVERNOR BENT HOUSE & MUSEUM 103

KIT CARSON HOUSE MUSEUM 107
LAS PALOMAS DE TAOS ADOBE 109
THE GARDEN RESTAURANT & BAKERY .. 112
THE HISTORIC TAOS INN 115
HACIENDA DEL SOL 119
THE ALLEY CANTINA 121
CHAPTER FOUR 122
FARMINGTON, NEW MEXICO 122
LIONS WILDERNESS PARK 124
CHAPTER FIVE 125
CHAMA, NEW MEXICO 125
FOSTER'S HOTEL RESTAURANT AND
SALOON 125
CHAPTER SIX 127
ESPANOLA, NEW MEXICO 127
ESPANOLA POLICE STATION 127
CHAPTER SEVEN CLOVIS, NEW MEXICO 129
NORMAN PETTY RECORDING STUDIOS ... 131
CHAPTER EIGHT 143
GALLUP, NEW MEXICO 143
OLD HOUSE ON AZTEC 144
EL RANCHO HOTEL 145
CHAPTER NINE 149
CONCLUSION 149
INDEX 151

CHAPTER ONE
THE LAND OF ENCHANTMENT

New Mexico has long been known as the Land of Enchantment and certainly is home to some of the strangest mysteries to be found in North America. As if New Mexico's known history is not fascinating enough, there is also the hidden history that is normally the fodder for conspiracy theories of one type of another. There have been stories coming out of this state about everything from crashed UFOs and recovered alien bodies to vast treasures being hidden in remote parts of the state. No matter which brand of conspiracy theory someone may adhere to, there is something related that can be found in the state of New Mexico

UNDERGROUND ALIEN BASES?

Certainly no book on New Mexico would be complete without at least touching on all of the many stories about secret underground alien bases that are supposed to be hidden around the state.

Buried deep in the desert near Dulce, New Mexico are caverns allegedly populated by aliens. Numerous abductees have reported being taken to the base to be examined, and most have seen members of various branches of our military, primarily United States Air Force personnel interacting with these mysterious aliens. According to some reports, the aliens are carrying on genetic experimentations, in secret agreement with our government.

In 1969, according to ex-Naval Intelligence Officer Milton Cooper, a confrontation took place inside the Dulce underground complex between the aliens and our own scientist in which 60 humans were killed. According to Mr. Cooper, elements of Delta Force were alleged to have been involved in this altercation. This site is said to be connected to the installation at Los Alamos and accessed by a secret underground shuttle system.

However, let me stress that the U.S. government, especially the United States Air Force, denies any knowledge of any alien base, joint genetic experiments, or any deaths of either civilian and/or military personnel connected to this perhaps, non-existent base.

However, when this writer went to Dulce in pursuit of Sasquatch in 2015, his guide, and several other members of the Jicarilla Apache Tribe were adamant that there was a concealed military installation on top of Archuleta Mesa. We did notice a flight of the mysterious black helicopters pass over the town of Dulce and disappear over the Mesa.

However, and with that being said, consider the following which came from a website called ABOVE TOP SECRET.COM[1]. On the home page of this very interesting website is an expose' regarding the alleged underground alien base located at Dulce, New Mexico.

EXTRA-TERRESTRIAL INSTALLATION IN DULCE, NEW MEXICO

THE FOLLOWING MATERIAL COMES FROM PEOPLE WHO KNOW THE DULCE (UNDERGROUND) BASE EXISTS. THEY ARE PEOPLE WHO WORKED IN THE LABS; ABDUCTEES TAKEN TO THE BASE; PEOPLE WHO ASSISTED IN THE CONSTRUCTION; INTELLIGENCE PERSONAL (NSA, CIA ,FBI etc.) AND UFO / INNER-EARTH RESEARCHERS.

---

[1] http://www.abovetopsecret.com/pages/dulce.html.

Located almost two miles beneath Archuleta Mesa on the Jicarilla Apache Indian Reservation near Dulce, New Mexico is an installation classified so secret, its existence is one of the least known in the world. Here is Earth's first and main joint United States Government/alien biogenetics laboratory. Others exist in Colorado, Nevada, and Arizona.

The multi-level facility at Dulce goes down for at least seven known levels, and is reported to have a central HUB which is controlled by base security. The level of security required to access different sections rises as one goes further down the facility. There are over 3000 real-time video cameras throughout the complex at high-security locations (entrances and exits). There are over 100 secret exits near and around Dulce. Many of the secret entrances are around Archuleta Mesa, while others to the south around Dulce Lake and some are even as far east as Lindrith. Deep sections of the complex also connect into natural cavern systems that underlie this region.

THE GREY SPECIES

Most of the aliens reside on sub-levels 5, 6, and 7 with alien housing on level 5. The alien species that controls the majority of the complex are the Greys, a devious race, now considered an enemy of the New World Order.

In the Fifties, the Greys began taking large numbers of humans for experiments. By the Sixties, the rate was speeded up and they began getting careless and self-involved. By the Seventies, their true intentions became very obvious, but the "Special Group" of the Government still kept covering up for them. By the Eighties, the Government realized there was no defense against the Greys. So, programs were enacted to prepare the public for open contact with non-human ET beings.

Perhaps there is a possible ally for the Human Race, the Reptoids, which is an enemy species of the Greys and as a result their relationship is in a constant state of tension. The Greys only known enemy is the Reptillian Race, and they are on their way to Earth.

A man named Thomas C., famous for stealing the so-called "Dulce Papers", says that there are over 18,000 short "greys" at the Dulce facility. He also has stated how a colleague of his had come face-to-face with a 6-foot tall Reptoid that had materialized in his house. The Reptoid showed a great interest in research maps of New Mexico and Colorado that were on the wall. The maps were full of colored pushpins and markers to indicate sites of animal mutilations, caverns, locations of high UFO activity, repeated flight paths, abduction sites, ancient ruins, and suspected alien underground bases.

Some forces in the Government want the public to be aware of what is happening. Other forces (The Collaborators) want to continue making "whatever deals are necessary" for an Elite few to survive the conflicts.

CLONING HUMANS (BY HUMANS) FOR SLAVE HYBRIDS

The Secret Government cloned humans by a process perfected in the world's largest and most advanced bio-genetic research facility, Los Alamos. The elite humans now have their own disposable slave-race. Like the alien Greys, the US Government secretly impregnated females, and then removed the hybrid fetus after a three month time period, before accelerating their growth in laboratories. Biogenetic (DNA Manipulation) programming is then instilled - they are implanted and controlled at a distance through RF (Radio Frequency) transmissions.

Many Humans are also being implanted with brain transceivers. These act as telepathic communication "channels" and telemetric brain manipulation devices. This network was developed and initiated by DARPA. Two of the procedures were RHIC (Radio-Hypnotic Intercerebral Control) and EDOM (Electronic Dissolution of Memory).

They also developed ELF and EM wave propagation equipment which affect the nerves and can cause nausea, fatigue, irritability, even death. This research into biodynamic relationships within organisms has produced a technology that can change the genetic structure and heal.

OVERT AND COVERT RESEARCH

U.S. Energy Secretary John Herrington named the Lawrence Berkeley Laboratory and New Mexico's Los Alamos National Laboratory to house new advanced genetic research centers as part of a project to decipher the human genome. The genome holds the genetically coded instructions that guide the transformation of a single cell, a fertilized egg, into a biological organism.

"The Human Genome Project may well have the greatest direct impact on humanity of any scientific initiative before us today", said David Shirley, Director of the Berkeley Laboratory.

Covertly, this research has been going on for years at the Dulce bio-genetics labs. Level 6 is hauntingly known by employees as "Nightmare Hall". It holds the genetic labs at Dulce. Reports from workers, who have seen bizarre experimentation, are as follows:

"I have seen multi-legged 'humans' that look like half-human/half-octopus. Also reptilian-humans, and furry creatures that have hands like humans and cries like a baby, it mimics human words... also huge mixture of lizard-humans in cages. There are fish, seals, birds and mice that can barely be considered those species. There are several cages (and vats) of winged-humanoids, grotesque bat-like creatures...but 3 1/2 to 7 feet tall. I have also seen Gargoyle-like beings and Draco-Reptoids."

"Level 7 is worse, row after row of thousands of humans and human mixtures in cold storage. Here too are embryo storage vats of humanoids in various stages of development. I frequently encountered humans in cages, usually dazed or drugged, but sometimes they cried and begged for help. We were told they were hopelessly insane, and involved in high risk drug tests to cure insanity. We were told to never try to speak to them at all. At the beginning we believed that story. Finally in 1978 a small group of workers discovered the truth. It began the Dulce Wars".

When the truth was evident that humans were being produced from abducted females, impregnated against there will, a secret resistance group formed. This did little though, over time they were assassinated or "died under mysterious circumstances".

As previously stated, there are over 18,000 "aliens" at the Dulce complex. In late 1979, there was a confrontation, primarily over weaponry and the majority of human scientists and military personnel were killed. The facility was closed for a while, but is currently active.

Human and animal abductions slowed in the mid-1980s, when the Livermore Berkeley Labs began production of artificial blood for Dulce. William Cooper states: "A clash occurred where in 66 people, of our people, from the National Recon Group, the DELTA group, which is responsible for security of all alien connected projects, were killed."

Members of the DELTA Group (within Intelligence Support Activity) have been seen with badges which have a black Triangle on a red background. DELTA is the fourth letter of the Greek alphabet. It has the form of a triangle, and figures prominently in certain Masonic Signs. EACH BASE HAS ITS OWN SYMBOL. The Dulce Base symbol is a triangle with the Greek letter "Tau" (T) within it and then the symbol is inverted, so the triangle points down.

The Insignia of "a triangle and 3 lateral lines" has been seen on "Saucer (transport) Craft", The Tri-Lateral Symbol. Other symbols mark landing sights and alien craft.

INSIDE THE DULCE COMPLEX

Security Officers wear jumpsuits, with the Dulce Symbol on the front upper left side. The standard hand weapon at Dulce is a "Flash Gun", which is good against humans and aliens. The ID card (used in card slots, for the doors and elevators) has the Dulce Symbol above the ID photo. "Government Honchos" use cards with the Great Seal of the U.S. on it, stating the words New World Order in Latin.

After the second Level, everyone is weighed in the nude, and then given a uniform. Visitors are given an 'off white' uniform. In front of ALL sensitive areas are scales built under the doorway, by the door control. The person's card must match with the weight and code or the door won't open. Any discrepancy in weight (any change over three pounds) will summon security. No one is allowed to carry anything into or out of sensitive areas. All supplies are put through a security conveyor system. The Alien Symbol language appears a lot at the Facility.

During the construction of the facility (which was done in stages, over many years) the aliens assisted in the design and construction materials. Many of the things assembled by the workers were of a technology they could not understand, yet it would function when fully put together. Example: The elevators have no cables. They are controlled magnetically. The magnetic system is inside the walls.

There are no conventional electrical controls. All is controlled by advanced magnetism. That includes a magnetically induced (phosphorescent) illumination system. There are no regular light bulbs. All exits are magnetically controlled. It has been reported that, "If you place a large magnet on an entrance, it will affect an immediate interruption. They will have to come out and reset the system."

MIND MANIPULATION EXPERIMENTS

Dulce has studied mind control implants, Bio-Psi Units, ELF devices capable of mood, sleep and heartbeat control.

DARPA is using these technologies to manipulate people. They establish 'The Projects', set priorities, coordinate efforts and guide the many participants in these undertakings. Related projects are studied at Sandia Base by "The Jason Group" (of 55 scientists). They have secretly harnessed the dark side of technology and hidden the beneficial technology from the public.

Other projects take place at the Groom Lake installation in Nevada, also known as Area 51. These projects include studies in: ELMINT (Electro-Magnetic Intelligence), Code Empire, Code Eva, Program His (Hybrid Intelligence System), BW/CW, IRIS (Infrared Intruder System), BI-PASS, REP-TILES.

The studies on Level 4 at Dulce include Human-Aura research, as well as all aspects of dreams, hypnosis and telepathy. They know how to manipulate the bioplasmic body of humans. They can lower your heartbeat, with deep sleep-inducing delta waves, induce a static shock, and then re-program via a neurological-computer link. They can introduce data and programmed reactions into your mind (information impregnation - the "Dream Library").

We are entering an era of the technologicalization of psychic powers. The development of techniques to enhance man/machine communications, nanotechnology, bio-technological micro-machines, PSI-War, E.D.O.M. (Electronic Dissolution of Memory), R.H.I.C. (Radio-

Hypnotic Intra-Cerebral Control) and various forms of behavior control (by chemical agents, ultrasonics, optical and other forms of EM radiation).

Is there a secret underground base in or around Dulce, New Mexico? I do not have an answer to that question, at least as of yet. This would certainly be an exciting topic for a new book about some of the mysteries of New Mexico. However, in the interim, let us look at another fascinating aspect of New Mexico's hidden history. This topic would be the very famous, or infamous crash of a UFO at Roswell, New Mexico.

THE CRASH AT ROSWELL, NEW MEXICO

According to all reports, in 1947 something crashed or was shot down just outside of Roswell, New Mexico. This incident has caused more controversy as to what really happened than most other UFO events in current history. According to many researchers, agents of the United States government came in and removed a mysterious craft and perhaps some alien bodies.

Rancher Mac Brazel reported finding portions of a crashed UFO on his ranch. The sheriff of Chaves County passed this information along to officials at Roswell Army Air Field (RAAF) and an investigation into the reported debris was begun by Maj. Jesse Marcel, an intelligence officer at the base.

A press release was issued by RAAF about the flying saucer on July 8, 1947. The following day, the official story was changed by Army Air Force officials. (Both stories were reported in front page articles in the Roswell Daily Record.) This Roswell Daily Record web site lets you explore the various reports on what has been termed the "Roswell Incident," a subject that has generated many news reports, books and motion pictures[2].

Roswell Daily Record for July 8, 1947

The intelligence office of the 509th Bombardment group at Roswell Army Air Field announced at noon today, that the field has come into possession of a flying saucer.

According to information released by the department, over authority of Maj. J. A. Marcel, intelligence officer, the disk was recovered on a ranch in the Roswell vicinity, after an unidentified rancher had notified Sheriff Geo. Wilcox, here, that he had found the instrument on his premises.

---

[2] http://www.crystalinks.com/newmexico.html

Major Marcel and a detail from his department went to the ranch and recovered the disk, it was stated.

After the intelligence officer here had inspected the instrument it was flown to higher headquarters. The intelligence office stated that no details of the saucer's construction or its appearance had been revealed.

Mr. and Mrs. Dan Wilmot apparently were the only persons in Roswell who saw what they thought was a flying disk.

They were sitting on their porch at 105 South Penn. last Wednesday night at about ten o'clock when a large glowing object zoomed out of the sky from the southeast, going in a northwesterly direction at a high rate of speed.

Wilmot called Mrs. Wilmot's attention to it and both ran down into the yard to watch. It was in sight less then a minute, perhaps 40 or 50 seconds, Wilmot estimated.

Wilmot said that it appeared to him to be about 1,500 feet high and going fast. He estimated between 400 and 500 miles per hour.

In appearance it looked oval in shape like two inverted saucers, faced mouth to mouth, or like two old type washbowls placed, together in the same fashion. The entire body glowed as though light were showing through from inside, though not like it would inside, though not like it would be if a light were merely underneath.

From where he stood Wilmot said that the object looked to be about 5 feet in size, and making allowance for the distance it was from town he figured that it must have been 15 to 20 feet in diameter, though this was just a guess.

Wilmot said that he heard no sound but that Mrs. Wilmot said she heard a swishing sound for a very short time.

The object came into view from the southeast and disappeared over the treetops in the general vicinity of six mile hill.

Wilmot, who is one of the most respected and reliable citizens in town, kept the story to himself hoping that someone else would come out and tell about having seen one, but finally today decided that he would go ahead and tell about it. The announcement that the RAAF was in possession of one came only a few minutes after he decided to release the details of what he had seen.

Roswell Daily Record for July 9, 1947 - AP

An examination by the army revealed last night that mysterious objects found on a lonely New Mexico ranch was a harmless high-altitude weather balloon - not a grounded flying disk. Excitement was high until Brig. Gen. Roger M. Ramey, commander of the Eighth air forces with headquarters here cleared up the mystery.

The bundle of tinfoil, broken wood beams and rubber remnants of a balloon were sent here yesterday by army air transport in the wake of reports that it was a flying disk.

But the general said the objects were the crushed remains of a ray wind target used to determine the direction and velocity of winds at high altitudes.

Warrant Officer Irving Newton, forecaster at the army air forces weather station here said, "We use them because they go much higher than the eye can see."

The weather balloon was found several days ago near the center of New Mexico by Rancher W. W. Brazel. He said he didn't think much about it until he went into Corona, N. M. last Saturday and heard the flying disk reports.

He returned to his ranch, 85 miles northwest of Roswell, and recovered the wreckage of the balloon, which he had placed under some brush.

Then Brazel hurried back to Roswell, where he reported his find to the sheriff's office.

The sheriff called the Roswell air field and Maj. Jesse A. Marcel, 509th bomb group intelligence officer was assigned to the case.

Col. William H. Blanchard, commanding officer of the bomb group, reported the find to General Ramey and the object was flown immediately to the army air field here.

Ramey went on the air here last night to announce the New Mexico discovery was not a flying disk.

Newton said that when rigged up, the instrument "looks like a six-pointed star, is silvery in appearance and rises in the air like a kite."

In Roswell, the discovery set off a flurry of excitement.

Sheriff George Wilcox's telephone lines were jammed. Three calls came from England, one of them from The London Daily Mail, he said.

A public relations officer here said the balloon was in his office "and it'll probably stay right there."

Newton, who made the examination, said some 80 weather stations in the U. S. were using that type of balloon and that it could have come from any of them.

He said he had sent up identical balloons during the invasion of Okinawa to determine ballistics information for heavy guns.

Story 2

W. W. Brazel, 48, Lincoln county rancher living 30 miles south of Corona, today told his story of finding what the army at first described as a flying disk, but the publicity which attended his find caused him to add that if he ever found anything else short of a bomb, he sure wasn't going to say anything about it.

Brazel was brought here late yesterday by W. E. Whitmore, of radio station KGFL, had his picture taken and gave an interview to the Record and Jason Kellahin, sent here from the Albuquerque bureau of the Associated Press to cover the story. The picture he posed for was sent out over AP telephoto wire sending machine specially set up in the Record office by R. D. Adair, AP wire chief sent here from Albuquerque for the sole purpose of getting out his picture and that of sheriff George Wilcox, to whom Brazel originally gave the information of his find.

Brazel related that on June 14 he and an 8-year old son, Vernon, were about 7 or 8 miles from the ranch house of the J. B. Foster ranch, which he operates, when they came upon a large area of bright wreckage made up on rubber strips, tinfoil, a rather tough paper and sticks.

At the time Brazel was in a hurry to get his round made and he did not pay much attention to it. But he did remark about what he had seen and on July 4 he, his wife, Vernon and a daughter, Betty, age 14, went back to the spot and gathered up quite a bit of the debris.

The next day he first heard about the flying disks, and he wondered if what he had found might be the remnants of one of these.

Monday he came to town to sell some wool and while here he went to see Sheriff George Wilcox and "whispered kinda confidential like" that he might have found a flying disk.

Wilcox got in touch with the Roswell Army Air Field and Maj. Jesse A. Marcel and a man in plain clothes accompanied him home, where they picked up the rest of the pieces of the "disk" and went to his home to try to reconstruct it.

According to Brazel they simply could not reconstruct it at all. They tried to make a kite out of it, but could not do that and could not find any way to put it back together so that it could fit.

Then Major Marcel brought it to Roswell and that was the last he heard of it until the story broke that he had found a flying disk.

Brazel said that he did not see it fall from the sky and did not see it before it was torn up, so he did not know the size or shape it might have been, but he thought it might have been about as large as a tabletop. The balloon which held it up, if that was how it worked, must have been about 12 feet long, he felt, measuring the distance by the size of the room in which he sat. The rubber was smoky gray in color and scattered over an area about 200 yards in diameter.

When the debris was gathered up the tinfoil, paper, tape, and sticks made a bundle about three feet long and 7 or 8 inches thick, while the rubber made a bundle about 18 or 20 inches long and about 8 inches thick. In all, he estimated, the entire lot would have weighed maybe five pounds.

There was no sign of any metal in the area which might have been used for an engine and no sign of any propellers of any kind, although at least one paper fin had been glued onto some of the tinfoil.

There were no words to be found anywhere on the instrument, although there were letters on some of the parts. Considerable scotch tape and some tape with flowers printed upon it had been used in the construction.

No strings or wire were to be found but there were some eyelets in the paper to indicate that some sort of attachment may have been used.

Brazel said that he had previously found two weather observation balloons on the ranch; but that what he found this time did not in any way resemble either of these.

"I am sure that what I found was not any weather observation balloon," he said. "But if I find anything else besides a bomb they are going to have a hard time getting me to say anything about it."

OTHER UFOS SPOTTED IN SOUTHWEST

I do not know if a UFO crashed at Roswell in 1947, but I do know that UFOs and their activities continue to be an area of major concern to both the United States government as well as that of Mexico. Consider if you will the following news story that made major headlines in 2004[3].

---

[3] http://www.wired.com/news/technology/0%2C1282%2C63433%2C00.html?tw=wn_tophead_9

MEXICAN AIR FORCE FILMS UFOS

Associated Press

11:17 AM May. 12, 2004 PT

Mexican Air Force pilots filmed 11 unidentified flying objects in the skies over southern Campeche State, a spokesman for Mexico's Defense Department confirmed Tuesday.

A videotape made widely available to the news media on Tuesday shows the bright objects, some sharp points of light and others like large headlights, moving rapidly in what appears to be a late-evening sky.

The lights were filmed on March 5 by pilots using infrared equipment. They appeared to be flying at an altitude of about 11,500 feet, and reportedly surrounded the jet as it conducted routine anti-drug trafficking vigilance in Campeche. Only three of the objects showed up on the plane's radar.

"Was I afraid? Yes. A little afraid because we were facing something that had never happened before," said radar operator Lt. German Marin in a taped interview made public Tuesday.

"I couldn't say what it was ... but I think they're completely real," added Lt. Mario Adrian Vazquez, the infrared equipment operator. Vazquez insisted that there was no way to alter the recorded images.

The plane's captain, Maj. Magdaleno Castanon, said the military jets chased the lights "and I believe they could feel we were pursuing them."

When the jets stopped following the objects, they disappeared, he said.

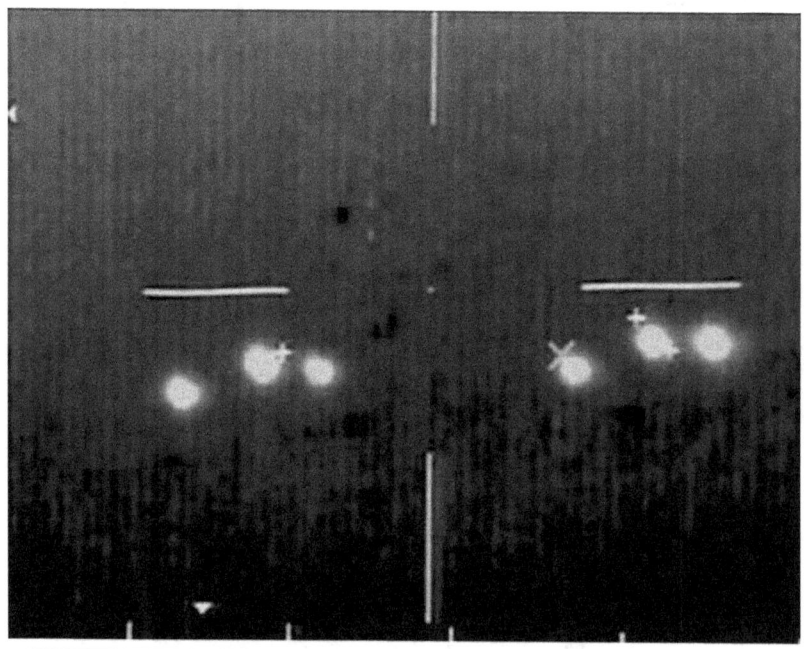

Figure 1: This is a photo taken by one of the planes.

A Defense Department spokesman confirmed Tuesday, that the videotape was filmed by members of the Mexican Air Force. The spokesman, who spoke on the condition of anonymity, declined to comment further.

The video was first aired on national television Monday night then again at a news conference Tuesday by Jaime Maussan, a Mexican investigator who has dedicated the past 10 years to studying UFOs.

"This is historic news," Maussan told reporters. "Hundreds of videos (of UFOs) exist, but none had the backing of the armed forces of any country.... The armed forces don't perpetuate frauds."

Maussan said he obtained the video from Secretary of Defense Gen. Ricardo Vega Garcia.

THE "OTHER" UFO CRASH IN NEW MEXICO

Much less well known than the famous Roswell UFO crash incident, there was said to be a crash of a UFO at the little town of Aztec, New Mexico.

According to the reports, on March 25, 1948, radar at Muroc Air Force Base in California and at two installations in Colorado tracked an object over the state of New Mexico as it came down and apparently crashed. By using triangulation, the military was able to narrow the site where it came to earth to an area 12 miles east of Aztec, New Mexico.

The military alerted local authorities, who immediately secured the area. General George C. Marshall,

Secretary of State, ordered a search party sent in from Camp Hale in Colorado. The helicopter team located the crash site on a rocky plateau. The object was a saucer about thirty feet in diameter, and it was undamaged except for a small hole in one of its portholes.

Scientists, including Dr. Carl Heiland of the Colorado School of Mines, Dr. Horace van Valkenberg of The University of Colorado, and Dr. Detlev Bronk, met at Durango, Colorado and were flown to the crash site.

Through the hole, the assembled group of scientists, led by a mysterious Dr. Gee, could see sixteen small but perfectly formed humanoids. All were dead, their skin brown as if having been burned. Since the only damage to the craft was the hole, it was theorized that a meteorite had hit the craft, making the hole, and "burning" the occupants by rapid decompression.

After trying to open hatches, and failing to cut or burn through the hull, the military stuck a long pole through the hole in the porthole and, while probing around with it, accidentally hit a control that opened a door.

The scientists entered the ship and brought out the sixteen bodies and laid them on the ground near the ship. Dr. Gee studied the bodies and found that every one had perfect teeth, that they were between thirty-five and forty, and that they probably came from Venus. They were all between thirty-six and forty-two inches tall, and they ate small wafers and drank water that was twice as heavy as Earth water. They wore clothing that was almost indestructible.

Measurements of the craft showed that it was 99.99 feet in diameter, 18 feet across, and 72 inches high. Several booklets filled with pictograms were found in the ship. Dr. Gee determined that the craft flew by jumping from one magnetic line of force to the next, there being 1,257 of these lines per square centimeter.

The ship and occupants were taken to Muroc Air Force Base, where President Eisenhower flew in to see them. After that, they were taken to Wright-Patterson Air Force Base near Dayton, Ohio.

Dr. Gee was privileged to examine another craft that landed in an Arizona desert near a proving ground, also 72 feet across and containing 16 dead aliens. The occupants had died when they opened the door and were exposed to Earth's atmosphere.

Finally, he had examined another craft that had landed in Paradise Valley, near Phoenix, Arizona. This craft was only 36 feet across and contained only two aliens. One had died sitting at the controls and the other was halfway out the hatch. Apparently they, too, had died when exposed to the air of this planet.

Dr. Gee told his friend Silas M. Newton about the crashes and gave him some small metallic discs taken from one of the ships. Newton, a millionaire oilman who had rediscovered the Rangely oil field by using microwaves, promptly scheduled a lecture on the crashes on March 8, 1950 at the University of Denver. Newton also talked to Variety columnist Frank Scully, who wrote about the crashes in his book Behind the Flying Saucers, published in September of 1950.

This was the basic story, but then it really gets mysterious. In 1952, a reporter named J.P. Cahn, on assignment for True magazine, investigated the story. He tracked down Newton and found that there was no evidence of his claim to having discovered oil fields using microwaves. Cahn was able to obtain one of the small metal discs that Newton claimed had come from one of the crashed UFOs and which he claimed would resist heat of 10,000 degrees. On analysis it turned out to be ordinary aluminum that would melt at 650 degrees. Cahn also located the mysterious "Dr. Gee", who turned out to be Leo Gebauer, an electrician who lived in Arizona. It was then believed that Newton and Gebauer were a couple of con men who had conned Frank Scully.

In October, 1974, Robert S. Carr, the southern director of NICAP (National Investigation Committee on Aerial Phenomenon) and also a former teacher at the University of South Florida resurrected the Aztec crash story.

In 1978, Flying Saucer Review published a paper by Leonard H. Stringfield that claimed Carr had eyewitness testimony to substantiate the Aztec crash. One was from a surgical nurse, now deceased (sound familiar?), who was said to have assisted in the autopsy of a dead alien. Carr would not give names, so none of his claims could be verified.

In 1986, William S. Steinman and Wendelle C Stevens reopened the case yet again with a book called UFO Crash at Aztec. The book was mostly speculation, but one of its sources was Dr. Robert Sarbacher, onetime consultant to the Research and Development Board, who said Scully's version of the Aztec crash, was "substantially correct." However, Sarbacher admitted that his information was secondhand.

In the early 1980s, William Moore investigated Silas M. Newton and Leo Gebauer and found that Newton was in trouble with the law as early as 1928, was charged in 1959 with selling worthless securities, was under indictment in 1970 for grand theft, and when he died in 1972, he had been charged with salting mines and oil wells to deceive investors. Gebauer had been investigated for violation of the White Slave Traffic Act, had been a Nazi sympathizer, and had at least a dozen aliases. He certainly wasn't a doctor.

Interviews with former (circa 1948) Aztec deputy sheriffs, newspaper editors, and townspeople, have found no evidence that a crash occurred there[4].

Of course, if as everyone maintains, the United States Government has a program of covering up such things as UFO crashes and alien bodies, then it is to be expected that a disinformation program would be instituted to discredit the story of a crash landing of a UFO at Aztec, New Mexico.

The most confusing aspect of trying to find out what happened is that when you begin to deal with UFOs and the "secret" government and the so called MJ-12 group, nothing is as it seems.

---

[4] Story by Roy Lawhon, http://ufos.about.com/od/ufocrashes/a/aa110704.htm.

The most bizarre part of this entire situation is that there is no absolute proof that a UFO crashed in either Roswell or in Aztec, but then again there is no proof that there were no crashes either. I guess the big question is how do you prove that something "Didn't" happen?

OTHER MYSTERIES

The question of whether or not UFOs crashed in New Mexico and the purported recovery of strange alien bodies is not the only mystery coming out of New Mexico. Alamogordo, New Mexico also has gone on record with sightings of some very strange aerial objects.

According to this story, strange green fire-balls that darted through the sky have been observed from the 1950's through the 1970's. A 'flap' of spectacular sightings occurred in 1957. Several of these unexplained sightings were reported over the Mescalero Apache Reservation in October of that year.

At 1:00 P.M. on November 4, a 'glowing oval object' flew over Highway 54 and caused automobiles to stall. The automobiles' lights, radios, and engines, all failed at the same time. An electronics engineer in one of the cars reported he felt 'waves of heat' as the object passed overhead. The exposed portions of his skin later became reddened and itchy.

At the same location, at 9:20 A.M. on November 7, a couple spotted an identical object and reported that their speedometer appeared to malfunction. All of the UFO reports led famous meteor researcher Dr. Lincoln La Paz to set up a research project to study them. Although the sightings of the 'fire-balls' or the 'objects' were never explained, the United States Air Force took an extreme interest in the project and treated 'them' very seriously.

Then the area of White Sands is also bothered with these pesky mystery lights. The White Sands area of New Mexico was a hotbed of missile testing in the 40s through the 60s. It was also a focal point of high UFO activity, particularly early on.

During a balloon launch on April 24, 1949, a General Mills engineer named Charles B. Moore Jr., along with four Navy personnel, witnessed a white spherical object in the sky. Moore had been looking for the balloon using a theodolite when he saw the UFO. He soon saw that it was more elliptical than round and that it seemed to be pursuing his balloon. This sighting later became a Blue Book "Unknown."

On June 10th, two more circular UFOs were sighted in the area. During a missile launch, the two objects were seen circling and passing through the weapon's exhaust, though the rocket was moving at 1430 mph. 5 tracking posts also confirmed having seen the objects.

In 1950, UFOs were finally caught on film, two times. On April 27, filming of a fallen missile also caught a UFO hovering nearby. Then, on May 29, two more UFOs were filmed moving at a speed of over 2000 mph.

More film was taken on July 14, 1951. During a test of the F-86 jet, several UFOs were seen and caught on film. The objects also appeared on radar.

UFO activity in the area still continued for years to follow and in fact there are a number of sightings almost every year.

Even the United States Air Force is not immune to these mysterious forces. At Kirtland Air Force in August through September of 1980 saw a series of alarming UFO incidents taking place near an active Air Force Base. Among the incidents were:

A UFO flying over a weapons storage area maneuvering in ways a helicopter could not.

A disk-shaped object near the ground behind an "alarmed structure," viewed by a former helicopter mechanic.

A craft landing in a restricted test range.

Air Force Radar Approach Control equipment and scanner radar were rendered inoperative by "high frequency jamming from an unknown cause." A thorough check in the area resulted in no answers.

According to the government document related to the incidents acquired through the Freedom of Information Act, the conclusion of the case, especially the latter jamming, included the terse comment: "The presence of hostile intelligence jamming cannot be ruled out." So who would have the power and ability to jam the Untied States Air Force?

Now we will turn our attention to an examination of more earthly mysteries such as ghosts and hauntings in Santa Fe and other towns in Northern New Mexico.

CHAPTER TWO
SANTA FE, NEW MEXICO

The area that is now the City of Santa Fe was originally occupied by a number of Pueblo Indian villages with founding dates between the years 1050 to 1150. The "Kingdom of New Mexico" was first claimed for the Spanish Crown by the conquistador Don Francisco Vasques de Coronado in 1540, 70 years before the founding of Santa Fe. Coronado and his men also traveled to the Grand Canyon and through the Great Plains on their New Mexico expedition.

Spanish colonists first settled in northern New Mexico in 1598. Don Juan de Oñate became the first Governor and Captain-General of New Mexico and established his capital in 1598 at San Juan Pueblo, 25 miles north of Santa Fe. When Oñate retired, Don Pedro de Peralta was appointed Governor and Captain-General in 1609. One year later, he moved the capital to present-day Santa Fe. New Mexico was part of the empire of New Spain and Santa Fe was the commercial hub at the end of the long road that linked Mexico City with its northern province.

During the next 70 years, Spanish soldiers and officials, as well as Franciscan missionaries, sought to subjugate and convert the Pueblo Indians of the region. The indigenous population at the time was close to 100,000 people, who spoke nine languages and lived in an estimated 70 pueblos, many of which exist today.

In 1680, Pueblo Indians revolted against some 2,500 Spanish colonists, killing 400 of them and driving the rest back into Mexico. The conquering Pueblos sacked Santa Fe and burned most of the buildings, except the Palace of the Governors. Pueblo Indians occupied Santa Fe until 1692-93, when Don Diego de Vargas reestablished Spanish control.

When Mexico gained its independence from Spain, Santa Fe became the capital of the province of New Mexico. Trade was no longer restricted as it was under Spanish rule and trappers and traders moved into the region. In 1821 William Becknell opened the 1,000 mile-long Santa Fe Trail.

On August 18, 1846, in the early period of the Mexican American War, an American army general, Stephen Watts Kearny, took Santa Fe and raised the

American flag over the Plaza. Two years later, 1848, Mexico signed the Treaty of Guadalupe Hidalgo ceding New Mexico and California to the United States.

In 1851, Vicar Apostolic, and later Archbishop of Santa Fe, Jean B. Lamy, arrived in Santa Fe. Eighteen years later, he began construction on the Saint Francis Cathedral, one of 45 churches he built in New Mexico. Built in the French Romanesque style, the building is alien to the Spanish heritage of Santa Fe, but is still one of its greatest landmarks. Constructed on the site of an adobe church destroyed in the Pueblo Revolt, the Cathedral was built of locally quarried stone. Portions of the old adobe parish church (La Parroquia), remain in the form of the Chapel of Our Lady of the Rosary, which houses a wooden stature of the Virgin know as La Conquistadora, Our Lady of the Conquest. La Conquistadora was first brought to Santa Fe in 1625 and was returned to the city by the armies of Don Diego de Vargas during the re-conquest of 1692-93.

For 27 days in March and April of 1862, the Confederate flag of Brigadier General Henry H. Sibley flew over Santa Fe until he was defeated by Union troops. With the arrival of the telegraph in 1868 and the coming of the Atchison, Topeka and the Santa Fe Railroad in 1880, Santa Fe and New Mexico underwent an economic revolution. Corruption in government, however, accompanied the growth, and President Rutherford B. Hayes appointed Lew Wallace as a territorial governor to "clean up New Mexico." Wallace did such a good job that Billy the Kid threatened to come up to Santa Fe and kill him.

New Mexico gained statehood in 1912 and Santa Fe has been the capital city since statehood.

Over ten years before the Plymouth Colony was founded by the Mayflower Pilgrims Santa Fe, New Mexico was established as the seat of power of the Spanish Empire north of the Rio Grande. Santa Fe is the oldest capital city in the United States and the oldest European community in the U.S. west of the Mississippi. The Palace of the Governors, on the north side of the Plaza, is the oldest public building in the United States. Santa Fe has been a seat of government under the flags of Spain, Mexico, the Confederacy, and the United States of America.

Courtesy of City of Santa Fe

THE GLOW HOUSE
Santa Fe, New Mexico

I was given this story by a friend who swore that it was true. According to his information, there is an abandoned church that the locals call "The Glow House." This little church was once headed by a priest who began to lose his mind as the number of parishioners that attended services began to shrink. The neighborhood was on a downward slide and the local kids were causing a great deal of mischief that was chasing away those that the priest looked on as his "flock". Blaming the local kids for his problems, the priest was especially annoyed by those children who continually disturbed the solitude of the church with the noise from the playground nearby.

One afternoon, the priest snapped and went on a killing rampage. He killed the children at the playground and hid their bodies in the basement of the old church. After a period of quiet repose, the priest regained his reason, the priest was so horrified by what he had done that he took his own life in atonement. Investigators later found the priest's body lying among the dead children.

It is said that there is a light that burns continually inside the church than does not go out. Strange sounds are heard from the old building and if someone tries to enter, a shadowy figure will chase them out and slam the door shut behind them.

THE COLLEGE OF SANTA FE
1600 St. Michael's Drive
Santa Fe, New Mexico

Figure 2: Library Building

The history of The College of Santa Fe dates to the days of the Old West. It was in 1859 that four Christian Brothers left France for Santa Fe at the request of Reverend J.B. Lamy, first bishop of New Mexico. They traveled for two months by boat, train, horseback and wagon train along the Santa Fe Trail to open a school for boys in Santa Fe.

St. Michael's College opened in impoverished conditions on Dec. 15, 1859. The Brothers taught in an adobe hut near the "oldest church" on the Pecos Trail (later College Street and today Old Santa Fe Trail). For a long time it was the sole source of education for boys in the Territory of New Mexico.

When the territory granted a charter to the "College of the Christian Brothers of New Mexico" in 1874, St. Michael's had expanded to include a program of higher education. At New Mexico's constitutional convention in 1910, 22 of the delegates (more than 20 percent of the convention) boasted St. Michael's as their alma mater. After World War I, however, the college program was dropped.

While St. Michael's continued to flourish as a preparatory school, the Christian Brothers dreamed of reinstating the collegiate program, bringing the option of independent higher education back to New Mexico. Through the efforts of Brother Benildus of Mary, their dreams came true in 1947 with the acquisition of the World War II Bruns Army Hospital on the edge of town. On Sept. 15, 1947, St. Michael's College (today's College of Santa Fe [5]) opened with 51 converted barrack buildings, 15 Christian Brothers serving as faculty members and 148 students.

---

[5] The College of Santa Fe is now the Santa Fe University of Art and Design.

In 1950 the College graduated its first class of 23. Upon the untimely death of Brother Benildus in 1957, Brother Raymond Ogden became acting president for one year. In 1958, Brother Cyprian Luke was appointed the College's third president. He led the institution as builder president. He led the institution as builder and innovative problem solver for 24 years until his retirement in June, 1982. There were many improvements during this growth period. After the achievement of accreditation in 1965, the student population, number of faculty and educational offerings increased rapidly.

In 1966 the name of the school was changed from St. Michael's College to The College of Santa Fe to show the close rapport between the school and the city it serves. The College began enrolling women that same year.

The College continued to evolve under the direction of Brother Donald Mouton, who was appointed by the Board of Trustees in 1982 as fourth president of the College. To meet the needs of local working adults, the Graduate and External Programs (GEP) division opened in 1980.

In 1985, the College's first graduate program, the Master of Business Administration, received accreditation from the North Central Association of Colleges and Schools.

One of the most significant changes was the College's expansion into Albuquerque following the closing of the University of Albuquerque in 1986. In a cooperative effort, the College agreed to assume the responsibility for programs of the University of Albuquerque to assure that students could complete their degrees. Today, the College of Santa Fe at Albuquerque continues to serve the community through two campus sites.

When Brother Donald Mouton resigned from the presidency of the College to return to teaching in December 1986, Dr. James Fries was selected as interim president. On June 5, 1987, the Board of Trustees appointed Dr. Fries president.

During President Fries' tenure, CSF has grown both academically and physically. A master's program in education was implemented, a new major in environmental science was started, and an exchange program with Universidad de La Salle in Mexico City was initiated.

Improvements at CSF continue to reflect social and student developments. The Lasallian philosophy of a caring, personalized education and a strong liberal arts curriculum remains unchanged.

THE GHOSTS

There are those who claim that there are a number of ghosts that haunt this campus. There is one ghost in particular who seems to be the best known. This figure is seen continually walking in the shadows late at night.

Another well-known ghost said to walk the halls of this institution of higher learning is that of a decapitated nurse that many students claim to have seen late at night.

According to the story, during World War II, an insane asylum was located in Bruns Army Hospital, the building that became the College of Santa Fe. During the time it was an Insane Asylum, it was reported that a patient suddenly went berserk, escaped form his room and went on a killing rampage. Before he could be restrained, the patient had cornered a nurse, cutting off her head with a fire axe. Now this decapitated nurse is sometimes seen walking in the hallways that lead to the cafeteria.

There is another story that was told to me on my last trip to Buffalo Thunder Casino for the Santa Fe Com-i-con. Apparently this story is on the Internet, though I have yet to look for it.

It seems that during World War II, several old unused barracks were moved onto the grounds of what was then the Bruns Army Hospital to expand the surgical facilities. When a military facility needed more space, it was customary to move in unused barracks as a quick fix.

Apparently these old barracks were used for a very long time. In fact, I was told that some of them are still in use today as office space. According to the story, one of the offices in the rear of the building was converted into a records holding area. I was told that like most records holding areas, the older records were simply stacked up.

Well, according to the story, one of the instructors had cause to enter the records holding area in search of a particular file. The lock was old and the key moved only stiffly in the lock. When the door was finally pushed open, there was the typical smell of musty papers and what was described as the smell of blood.

So the instructor stood there for a moment visually searching the room for some clue where to search for the file she needed. Like most seldom used records rooms, there were wall to wall filing cabinets, od desks and chairs and just hadn't been thrown out yet.

Finally, she found the particular file she needed and started for the door, but found that she was having trouble breathing. She paused to rest for a moment, suddenly overcome with the feeling that someone had actually died in that musty, hot storage room. Once she was out of the "death room", she made sure to never enter the room again.

GRANT CORNER INN
122 Grant Avenue
Santa Fe, New Mexico

The Grant Corner Inn is located in a very elegant three story colonial style home built in 1905 for Judge Arthur Robinson and his wife for many, many years. It was then used as an office building in the 1950s and became an inn in 1982. It is located in the heart of downtown Santa Fe. The Inn proper contains nine rooms that are furnished with antiques. According to the literature on this charming little hotel, it prides itself on its friendly, warm atmosphere. What is seldom mentioned is that in addition to the charm and antique furnishings, is that this old home also comes with a few spirits.

THE GHOSTS

Custodians, guests, and visitors have reported a number of ghostly encounters over the years. Unexplainable sounds of heavy objects falling to the floor, doors banging shut, and loud footsteps are heard throughout the building. Police have been called on several occasions.

According to all reports, rooms 4 and 8 and the hallway on the second floor are the primary haunting sites. There have been incidents of the sounds of heavy objects falling on the floor, footsteps, and slamming doors. Later investigations reveal nothing has fallen and no explanation for the footsteps or slamming doors. Some witnesses have claimed to have seen a grayish figure in the hallways that always seems to vanish right before their eyes.

In "Adobe Angels: Ghosts of Santa Fe and Taos," Antonio Garcez interviewed Art Garcia, former caretaker of this B&B. Garcia's account was terrifying — he endured deafening noises, a blast of freezing air that killed his house plants, the stench of rotting meat. He tried to convince friends to stay with him, only to have them leave hurriedly, frightened for their lives.

According to owner Louise Stewart, the spirit that haunted her house so violently has since quieted down. Extensive remodeling has been done since Stewart bought the building ("We gutted it," she says), and she thinks the unhappy spirit may have left.

Then again, maybe it's just waiting for the right guest to torment[6].

LA FONDA HOTEL
100 East San Francisco Street
Santa Fe, New Mexico

When Santa Fe was founded in 1607, official records show an inn or Fonda was among the first businesses established. More than two hundred years later, in 1821, when Captain William Becknell completed the first successful trading expedition from Missouri to Santa Fe - a route that came to be known as the Santa Fe Trail - he enjoyed the hospitality at the inn (la fonda), where the Santa Fe Trail terminated at the town's central Plaza.

The current La Fonda was built in 1922 on the site of the previous inns. In 1925 it was acquired by the Atchison, Topeka Santa Fe Railroad which leased it to Fred Harvey who operated it as one of his famous Harvey Houses. For more than 40 years, from 1926 to 1968, La Fonda was one of the more successful Harvey Houses, a renowned chain of fine hotels.

---

[6] Wheeler, Liza, <u>N.M. Has Its Share of Haunts</u>, Albuquerque Journal, Thursday, October 31, 2002.

Since 1968, La Fonda has been locally owned and operated and has continued the same tradition of providing warm hospitality, excellent service and modern amenities while maintaining historic integrity and architectural authenticity.

Throughout its long history, La Fonda has changed and evolved many times, but it continues to be the true heart of Santa Fe for visitors and locals alike.

THE GHOSTS

The present La Plazuela Dining Room in this lovely old hotel was originally an enclosed courtyard that was situated around an old well. Over 100 years ago, during the period of time in which a casino operated in this historic old building, a salesman who had a streak of bad luck and lost all of his company's money left the gambling tables and leapt to his death into the old well. From time to time, guests in the dining room sometimes report seeing a man walk to the center of the room and then jump as if into an invisible hole and simply disappear.

This building is old — it was already built when the city of Santa Fe was founded in the early 1600s. Alan Jordan, president of About Walks and Tours in Santa Fe, says that at one point, court was held in the building, and the public hangings of those found guilty took place in the lobby.

Besides the hangings (as if they weren't enough), there were plenty of other documented deaths in the La Fonda. In 1867, when La Fonda was known as the "Exchange Hotel," building records show Judge John P. Slough was killed in the lobby by Captain Rynerson, a member of the Territorial Legislature representing Dona Ana County. Rynerson shot him in the stomach after Slough called him a liar and a thief. He was later acquitted. Many people believe the judge still haunts the building today. The hotel archives also document the hanging death of some poor soul by a lynch mob in the hotel's back yard.[7]

LA RESIDENCIA
820 Paseo De Peralta
Santa Fe, New Mexico

La Residencia, located at the corner of Palace Avenue and Paseo de Peralta is a long term nursing facility that has been operated by Presbyterian Medical Services since late in 1983. On October 14, 2003, the facility closed its doors for the final time. The move meant the 101

---

[7] Ibid.

residents had to find new quarters within a short period of time and the 106 employees either had to look for new jobs or move into new quarters.

The facility that housed this nursing home was originally the site of the original St. Vincent Hospital, the Santa Fe community hospital.

THE GHOSTS

There are a number of former staff and, not a few residents, who talk of strange sounds coming from empty rooms as well as ghostly dark clad figures being glimpsed in the hallways at night. Others whisper of malevolent inhuman figures sticking their heads into rooms to glare at the terrified residents.

The muffled crying of a little boy who died in Room 311 when this as still the community hospital is still heard by nurses. The child and his father both died of injuries suffered in an automobile accident on Interstate 25. The eerie sounds from Room 311 are so frequent that the nursing home administrators try to keep the room unoccupied.

The hauntings of the upper floors seemed to be taken in stride by the nursing staff. However, almost all of them wanted nothing to do with the basement of the building. The staff was almost unanimous in their belief that something evil lurked in the darkened corridors of the bottom floor.

When the State Museum, which is located in the building next door, began storing Indian artifacts in part of the huge basement, some nurses absolutely refused to enter the area. Those that would speak of their experiences claimed that they saw shadowy figures moving about the hallways and heard strange sounds such as banging and voices talking rapidly emanate from the basement rooms.

As usually happens in every organization the old timers thought it was fun to require the newcomers to the staff to go through a "rite of passage" that required them to spend some time in the basement. One of the staff members would take the new employee to the basement on the elevator and then required the rookie to cross the darkened basement to the stairway and then ascend to the third floor.

However one evening, a new staff member, a very young, inexperienced, nurse's aide, was taken to the basement and given her assignment. The one that had taken her to the basement then returned to the third floor to await the rookie's arrival. Traditionally, the newcomer always arrived shortly with some truly bizarre stories of thinks in the dark. This time, the new staff member did not arrive via the stairs; in fact, she did not arrive at all.

Concerned that something had happened to the young girl, two nurses went to the dark basement to look for the nurse's aide. They searched the main part of the basement, but found no sign of the aide. Finally, in desperation, they begin to call her name. Finally, she answered, her voice faint and far away. With the aid of a flashlight, the two nurses finally located the newcomer, in a small dark room, far down one of the hallways, crouched in the corner.

The very scared young lady confessed that she had become disoriented in the dark and lost her way. When she heard something moving in the darkness, she had run until she found the small room in which she was hiding. The older nurse calmed the young aide and the two started for the door. Then they both froze – oozing down the wall beside the doorway of the small room was fresh blood. The nurse later said that it covered most of the wall and seemed to actually be coming from then wall. Not waiting to see anything else, the two ran for the elevator where the other nurse was holding the car.

Later, the nurses discovered that St. Vincent's had once had a small incinerator in that same room where hospital maintenance personnel had cremated amputated limbs.

LA POSADA DE SANTA FE
330 East Palace Avenue
Santa Fe, New Mexico

Located on land originally owned by one of Santa Fe's first families, the establishment now called the La Posada de Santa Fe Resort & Spa was long known as The Staab House, named after an early Santa Fe settler, Abraham Staab, who built the original mansion for his wife Julia. The original part of the hotel was originally the Staabs' Victorian mansion built in 1882.

Later the elegant structure was adobeized; in other words, an adobe structure was literally built around the original structure. Now the original Victorian presence is found only within the charming bar, the original staircase and four rooms upstairs, which still maintain the original brick and high ceilings.

It is said that Julia Staab, who died in 1896, continues to haunt the place. Mischievous but good-natured, Julia is said to be Santa Fe's best-known and most frequently witnessed ghost, normally seen on the second floor of the hotel in Room 256.

According to the hotel's archives, the house was built for her shortly after the Civil War by her husband, Abraham, who had amassed a fortune as a major supply contractor for the U.S. Army. Room 256 was originally Julia's bedroom in life and reflects much of its original charm. It is a large room, comprised of over 600 square feet and in keeping with the history of the room it is furnished with king sized brass bed, antique furniture and beautiful area rugs.

After the latest renovation of her former bedroom in the 1980s, Julia now seems to prefer the dining room on the second floor[8]. Staff members have reported that a strong gust of wind will blow through the room as they set the room up for parties. If there are candles burning on the table after the guests depart, somehow they are all extinguished. It would seem that even in death Julia Staab is a good and careful hostess.

One staff member was cleaning the floor in the dining room when he looked up to find Mrs. Staab standing nearby watching him work. He said that she had the most intense eyes he had ever seen.

---

[8] Norman, Michael and Beth Scott, <u>Haunted Heritage</u>, TOR, New York. 2002.

In an unidentified magazine clipping titled "The Ghost" that La Posada keeps in its archives, Mary Lee White writes that Julia Staab entertained endlessly and "was such a socialite that few recognized her dedication to her family." But after her infant son died of an illness, Julia's hair turned prematurely white. "People then realized," White writes, "that she was a sensitive and conscientious mother as well as a prominent wife, hostess and socialite."

White goes on to explain that many more unsuccessful pregnancies probably contributed to her early demise at age 52. The obituary that ran in The New Mexican gave scant details about the death.

"The official record contained nothing untoward about Mrs. Staab's demise," White writes. "But rumors afoot in Santa Fe had it that Julia had gone crazy and was kept in her room the last few years of her life."

Given the uncertainty surrounding Staab's death, it doesn't surprise some that her spirit seems to remain in her old house, interfering with La Posada's employees and guests.

Bartender Judy Vanderbeck says last Mother's Day, before a packed house, glasses flew off the shelf one by one, crashing to the floor; the fireplace kept turning on and off; and seasoned waitresses dropped trays as if someone pushed them up from underneath. Perhaps Julia Staab didn't go gently into her eternal sleep[9].

There may well be another ghost in residence at the La Posada De Santa Fe. One evening as a security guard was making his rounds; he heard the sound of a man's voice talking in the closed lounge area. He was unable to understand what was said, but there was no doubt that someone was talking. However, when he opened the door for a quick peek inside, the lounge was empty.

There is also other evidence regarding a male ghost in the hotel A young hotel guest awoke one night to see a man wearing a waistcoat standing over her bed. When she asked who he was, the man vanished.

Finally, an employee working in the hotel's office, which is off of the main lobby glanced up from her work to see a man standing by the front entrance. She looked back down at what she was doing and then realized that there was not supposed to be anyone in the lobby so late at night. When she looked back up, the man was gone. A search did not reveal anyone roaming the hallways or outside the front doors.

---

[9] Ibid.

Others have also heard pots and pans making noise in the empty kitchen as if someone was cooking. A heavy cut glass chandelier in one of the dining rooms will periodically begin to swing back and forth though no one or nothing is touching it. Then most unnerving of all, staff and guests alike have heard the sound of a woman sobbing that seems to come from everywhere in the old building.

SANTA FE INDIAN SCHOOL
1500 Cerrillos Road
Santa Fe, New Mexico

The federal government's treatment of the Native American tribes has been called nothing short of shameful. As if dealing with a defeated country, the United States government even went so far as to take the children of the Native Americans and send them to special schools designed to eradicate their native culture and replace it with the culture of main stream America. In many cases, Native American children were forcibly taken from their parents to be sent to these schools. Many of these unfortunate children died in these schools.

One such school was the Santa Fe Indian School which was founded in 1890 as a federal boarding school to culturally assimilate Indian children through education and isolation from their families. In 1962, the Santa Fe Indian School merged with the Albuquerque Indian School, and the Santa Fe site was taken over by the Institute of American Indian Arts. A series of events beginning in the mid-1970's led to the Albuquerque Indian School being transferred to the Santa Fe Indian School, and the Institute of American Indian Arts permanently relocating to a neighboring site in Santa Fe. As a result of the passage of the Indian Self Determination Act in 1975, administration of the school transferred from the U.S. Government to the American Indian Pueblo Council. The school has evolved into a community school with the missions of fostering traditional Indian culture, while teaching the skills necessary for students to thrive as individuals.

THE GHOSTS

There are those that believe that the Santa Fe Indian School is one of the most haunted places in New Mexico. The spirits that haunt this site are those of the young Native American children who were, sometimes, forcibly, taken from their homelands in the late 1800s to be taught in the Indian School system.

Over the many yeas that this school has been in existence, some of what are now dormitories were once hospitals where these Indian children were treated for illnesses, some buildings were churches where they were taught a new religion and sadly, some of these buildings were morgues where some children were taken who caught the dreaded small pox and died.

There are stories that the children who died of small pox were buried in one huge grave behind the track field and not sent home for fear that the rest of the tribes would be infected with this deadly disease. Many former students say that there are balls of light that can be seen jumping around behind the school. Others have been adamant that they have heard children's voices coming from the top floors of the dorms where no students are housed. Still others talk of things moving by themselves, radios changing, showers turning on, beds shaking and the unbelievably eerie feelings that they are not along when they have entered certain rooms.

Some also tell stories of seeing the shadows of bodies being hanging from the ceiling as if they had been hung and the sounds of voices screaming as if in agony.

PENITENTIARY OF NEW MEXICO, STATE FE
P.O. Box 1059
Santa Fe, New Mexico

The Main Unit of the Penitentiary of New Mexico at Santa Fe was opened in 1956 to house long term offenders. In 1980, there was a major rebellion at the New Mexico State Penitentiary, though it was said to have been an inmate rebellion without a plan, without leadership and without goals. Once the uprising began, a sort of mob mentality seemed to overcome the rioting inmates. There were few heroes, plenty of villains and many victims.

When State Police marched into the Penitentiary of New Mexico on Feb. 3, 1980, they didn't retake the prison from rioting inmates so much as they occupied the charred shell after the riot had burned itself out.

Thirty-three inmates were found dead inside -- some of them horribly butchered by their fellow prisoners. The emergency room at St. Vincent Hospital in Santa Fe was overwhelmed with more than 100 inmates -- some beaten, others suffering from drug overdoses. Eight of the 12 guards who had been taken hostage were treated for injuries, though, amazingly, none of the guards had been killed. It was a black mark on New Mexico history as the nation was captivated by the horror stories that dribbled out of Santa Fe.

The riot began in the early morning hours of Saturday, Feb. 2, when guards entered dormitory E-2 on the south side of the prison.

For some unknown reason, the door to the dormitory wasn't locked, in violation of prison security procedures. Neither was a hallway gate that led to the prison control room. Four guards were taken hostage during the first few minutes of the riot. In all, there were 15 guards on duty inside the prison that night, supervising more than 1,100 inmates.

Inmates rushed down the main corridor and broke the shatterproof glass at the control center. The guard on duty fled, leaving behind keys that could open most of the prison gates and doors.

Once the inmates assumed control of the cellblocks, the inside of the prison became a nightmare of violence. One Associated Press reporter later described it in a story distributed worldwide as a "merry-go-round gone crazy." A large number of fires were set as other inmates ripped out plumbing fixtures, flooding parts of the prison. Other inmates got into the infirmary and began taking drugs while still others began hunting their enemies and found them.

Sometime around 8 a.m. that Saturday morning, inmates began using tools from the prison to gain access to cellblock 4, which housed the "snitches" and inmates in protective segregation. The "snitches" housed in that cellblock all met a horrible end. One was hung from the upper tier of the cellblock, another decapitated. Most of the 33 inmates killed were from the segregation unit.

Early Saturday morning, fitful negotiations began with some inmate leaders. Ambulances shuttled the dead and injured to St. Vincent Hospital in Santa Fe. Smoke continued to pour out of the prison gymnasium.

It became clear later that neither the inmates nor the state had a single spokesman during the negotiations. This resulted in a great deal of confusion in the attempted negotiations. Eventually, however, the prison inmates made 11 basic demands. Some concerned basic prison conditions like overcrowding, inmate discipline, educational services and improving food. They also wanted outside witnesses to the negotiations such as federal officials and the news media.

Guards who had been taken hostage when the riot started were finally released. Some of the guards had been protected by inmates; others were brutally beaten. "One was tied to a chair. Another lay naked on a stretcher, blood pouring from a head wound," a Journal reporter wrote. Negotiations broke off about 1 a.m. Sunday and state officials insisted no concessions had been made. But the riot, fueled by drugs and hate, was running out of gas.

Later Sunday morning, inmates began to trickle out of the prison, seeking refuge at the fence where National Guardsmen stood with their M-16s. Black inmates led the exodus from the smoldering cellblocks, staying in groups large enough to defend themselves from other inmates. The largest riot in New Mexico Prison History was over.

THE GHOSTS

Many have said that violent emotion can produce hauntings and this prison riot released emotions that had been suppressed for years. Inmates went on a killing spree unprecedented in New Mexico prison history.

The most active areas of the prison are Cell Blocks 3, 4, the Tool room and the laundry room. Cell Block 3 was the maximum security ward which also contained the Solitary confinement cell. Some of the ghostly activity reported here includes unexplainable noises, doors that open and close by themselves, and lights that turn on and off without any apparent cause.

Cell block 4 was the area where the "snitches" and other prisoners held in protective custody were contained. Upon entering the cell block, there are marks on the floor where rioters used power tools to decapitate the snitches and several other inmates. Also visible are the outlines of scorch marks where other inmates were burned to death with propane cutting torches. Another inmate was hung from the upper tier of the cell block with sheets that had been tied together. The activity reported here is similar to those reported in Cell Block 3. Twenty three of the inmates that were murdered during the riot were killed in Cell Block 4.

The laundry was the site of several murders, although they occurred long before the riot of 1980. It is located in a labyrinth of corridors that lie underneath the prison. These corridors also link to the gas chamber, many mechanical rooms and the tool room where the inmates stole the propane torches and other tools that were used during the riots. Uneasy feelings and whispers are often reported down there as well as unusual human shaped shadows.

THE OLDEST HOUSE
215 East De Vargas Street
Santa FE, New Mexico.

The house at this address is said to be the oldest house in Santa Fe. If true, this would probably make it one of the oldest houses in the United States as Santa Fe is next to the oldest European settlement in the country.

According to legend, at one time this house was inhabited by two women who were said to be "brujas" or witches. Whether either of these two women were actual card carrying witches is not important, but they had gained a reputation for making a love potion that was said to be very effective. Most of the young men of wealth came to this house to purchase what they believed was the key to true love.

One young man came to see the two witches and purchased the love potion that had become so famous for paving the way for wealthy marriages in Santa Fe. He paid the price demanded by the two witches and received the potion. He then went to see the young woman he desired for his own and arranged for her to drink the potion. To his shock, even after drinking the magic potion that had been so successful for so many other suitors, the young woman chose to marry another man. The young suitor felt that he had been cheated.

The disappointed young man returned to the house on De Varas Street and demanded his money back. Apparently this conversation became very heated because one of the two women grabbed a large butcher knife and with one swing, separated the spurned suitor's head from his body.

It was said that the witches dumped the body and the head in the nearby Santa Fe River. Some have said that the spurned lover searches for his head as he can never know peace in death until his body is whole again. Though the body was found, the head was never recovered.

One of the streets that runs toward the Santa Fe River is called Alto Street. Not too much is known about this street that runs down toward the river. It is said that this street is haunted by the headless caballero. This cursed young man is said to brandishes a sword over where his head should be as he rides his phantom horse down the road to the Santa Fe River.

CASA REAL HEALTH CARE CENTER
501 Galisteo Street
Santa Fe, New Mexico

The Casa Real Health Care Center is a senior health-care facility that was built in 1985. In spite of the relatively new age of this building, it seems to have become endowed with the violent history of the ground upon which it was, perhaps unwisely, built. Of all of the things that contractors take into consideration when constructing a new facility, what might have previously occupied the land is certainly not of prime importance. In this case, perhaps, it should have been given more attention.

This building, designed to be a shelter and a place of care for the aged and the infirm was built on top of an old penitentiary graveyard next to another haunted building. Later happenings made it clear that something had lingered in the cemetery that found an outlet for its rage and violent emotions in the newly built Healthcare Center.

Employees, patients, and visitors to the 112-bed convalescent center have complained of an oppressive, uncomfortable feeling that seems to emanate from the place. The moment a person steps through the front door, they are assaulted by what seems to be waves of emotions.

Strange cold spots move through the rooms, and unexplained moaning sounds have been heard in the north and south wings.

THE SCHOOL OF AMERICAN RESEARCH
606 Garcia Street
Santa Fe, New Mexico

Figure 3: The Admin Building on the historic campus.

The historic campus of the School of American Research (SAR) is located on Santa Fe's east side. Built by sisters Amelia Elizabeth White and Martha Root White in the 1920s, the estate became the home of SAR in 1973. Canyon Road, with its many galleries and shops is within walking distance and the Santa Fe Plaza, the heart of the city, is one mile away[10].

Martha Root White and Amelia Elizabeth White were the very wealthy spinster daughters of the well known New York publisher Horace B. White. They were also two women with a love for the southwest in general and Santa Fe in particular. During the 1920s the two women came to Santa Fe and built an estate that they called El Dilirio[11].

In keeping with the lifestyle that they had become accustomed to while living in New York as the only children of Horace White, the two women made it a point to cultivate those in the arts living in Santa Fe. As a result, El Delirio became known as a popular gathering place for Santa Fe writers and artists. The two sisters were very generous supporters of the arts and were also among those who loved the art of the southwest Native Americans. The White sisters were the ones to open a gallery in New York City dedicated solely to the art of the Native Americans of the Southwest.

Martha White died in 1937, but Amelia Elizabeth White lived on at El Delirio until her own death in 1972 at the age of 96. No one was surprised when her will was

---

[10] http://www.sarweb.org/home/directions/directions.htm.
[11] Norman, Michael and Beth Scott, Haunted Heritage, TOR, New York. 2002.

read. She had stipulated that her estate and all of her other properties in and around Santa Fe be donated to the School of American Research.

The School of American Research was established in Santa Fe, New Mexico in 1907 as a center for the study of the archaeology and ethnology of the American Southwest. In the early years of the twentieth century, archaeology was a young discipline with roots in the art historical studies of Old World antiquities. The unveiling of the treasures of Troy, Ephesus, and the Valley of the Kings held the world spellbound.

In 1906 Alice Cunningham Fletcher, a pioneering anthropologist and ethnographer of Plains Indian groups, was on the American Committee of the Archaeological Institute of America. The AIA, founded in Boston in 1879, had schools in Athens, Rome, and Palestine that sponsored research into the foundations of classical civilization and promoted professional standards in archaeological field work. Fletcher wanted to establish an "Americanist" center with three aims: to train students in the profession of archaeology, to engage in anthropological research on the American continent, and to preserve and study the unique cultural heritage of the Southwest. Her aims coincided with those of Edgar Lee Hewett, an innovative educator and passionate amateur archaeologist whom she met in 1906 in Mexico.

Hewett, nicknamed "El Toro," was a flamboyant and controversial figure. He served as president of New Mexico Normal School in Las Vegas (now New Mexico Highlands University) from 1898 to 1903, where he taught some of the first courses in anthropology to be offered at any U.S. college. Hewett transformed himself from an amateur to a professional archaeologist, undertaking a doctoral program at the University of Geneva in 1903 and writing his dissertation, "Les Communautés Anciennes Dans le Desert Américain," on the distribution and social organization of archaeological peoples in the greater Southwest and northern Mexico. His work as a lobbyist for the protection of archaeological sites led to the creation of Mesa Verde National Park and the passage of the Preservation of American Antiquities Act of 1906.

In December of 1907 the American Committee of the AIA accepted Fletcher's plan to establish an American program and appointed Hewett the director of the new School of American Archaeology. Alice Fletcher was named the first chairperson of the School's managing committee. From this institutional base, Hewett became a key architect of the discipline of Southwestern archaeology over the next forty years.

THE GHOSTS

There are many stories both about the White sisters as well as the property upon which they built their famed estate. There are those who believe that El Delirio was built upon the site of an ancient Indian Pueblo. It is said that a number of relics found on the property from this ancient site are inside the mansion.

Additionally, there is no question that the White sisters were somewhat eccentric. The bodies of these two wealthy women are buried under a gazebo on the property as well as the bodies of some twenty rare Afghan and Irish wolfhounds raised by the sisters.

Whatever many be the cause, there is also no question that spirits roam this palatial estate. Some of the staff swears that late in the evenings, they have heard the voices of women talking outside the building. However, when they try to find the source of the conversations, there is never anyone found. On another occasion, an employee working late heard the front doorbell ring. She then heard the front door open and footsteps come down the hallway to the very room in which she was working. She heard the footsteps enter the room and then retreat back toward the front door and then the door open and close. During this entire time, she saw no one through the steps came to within a few feet of where she sat.

More than one person who has spent time in or around the gazebo beneath which the White sisters rest for all eternity report having felt like they are being watched even though they can find no one about. Perhaps the White Sisters are curious about the new comers using their beloved estate.

Another individual, a professor always felt as if someone was following her around and then reading over her shoulder as she worked though she never saw any sign of anyone. She would usually find her office door open when she knew very well that she had closed it the night before. Her dog also reacted as if there was someone in the room that had become her office that she was not able to see. Many times she found items in her office rearranged and the furniture showed signs of being cleaned; through no one would admit to cleaning her office.

Someone staying in what had been Amelia White's bedroom left for several days on vacation. Though the door had been locked when the occupant left, upon her return, she found the door open and the room had the appearance that it had been cleaned in her absence.

Finally, there is an arroyo near the school that has the reputation of being haunted. Many times, people have heard the sounds of conversations and laughter coming from this area, but they never find anyone that could account for the sounds.

LEGAL TENDER SALOON
Just off of Paseo de Peralta
Santa Fe, New Mexico

This historic old building was built in 1881 and has been used for a number of purposes over the years. Of course, being located across the street from the train depot, it was a natural spot for a commercial establishment. The first of these ventures was first called the Pflueger General Merchandise Store and Annex Saloon. It is also known that after serving its time as a general retail establishment and a bar that it became a vaudeville house for a time.

Then in the 1950s, the building was home to the Pink Garter and then in 1969, it became known as the Legal Tender Saloon and Restaurant.

THE GHOSTS

This old saloon and vaudeville hall is said to be haunted by several ghosts.

First, there is a lady dressed in an elegant white gown who is seen floating up the steps to the balcony in the Parlor Room. No one seems to know her identity. There is also a little girl ghost in a long dress that sits all alone on the stairs. She looks so lonely that a lot of kind hearted people who do not realize that she is a ghost try to comfort her, but if anyone approaches her, she fades slowly away.

There is also a man dressed all in black who had the misfortune to be killed by a stray bullet fired in the rowdy gambling hall. This gentleman has been seen helping himself to a drink at the bar. Once again, no one seems to know who this mysterious figure might be.

NIGHT SKY GALLERY
826 Canyon Road
Santa Fe, New Mexico

This one-story building is now the fashionable Night Sky Gallery catering to the artsy crowd in Santa Fe. It is also said that this building has long been haunted by strange voices and unexplainable sounds for many years. Gentle voices are heard during the winter months carrying on conversations though no one is seen. Many who have visited this building that have heard the voices say that they have experienced feelings of tremendous fear. According to director Kate Norton, there is an uneasy feeling about the place after hours, and employees refuse to spend the night in the building.

ST. VINCENT HOSPITAL
Santa Fe. New Mexico

St. Vincent Hospital, established in 1865, has been caring for the communities of Santa Fe and northern New Mexico for more than 150 years. Originally run by the Sisters of Charity, today's St. Vincent is a non-profit, non-affiliated hospital with a board of directors.

Many things have changed since the hospital opened its doors in 1865, but its mission remains the same, to care for all the people of Santa Fe, northern New Mexico, and southern Colorado regardless of their ability to pay.

THE GHOSTS

The ghost of a very short Hispanic man dressed in old fashioned clothing, appeared several times to a nurse on the top floor of this three-story modern hospital. The ghost of a woman wearing a black mantilla was observed with the man. The ghostly couple seemed confused and in need of some kind of help. The hospital was built in 1977 on top of an old penitentiary graveyard. A more recent hospital operated on this same tract of land also reported paranormal activity.

THREE SISTERS BOUTIQUE
211 Old Santa Fe Trail
Santa Fe. New Mexico

Years ago, the Sisters of Loretto operated a Catholic school in the area that is now occupied by the Inn of Loretto. Nearby there is a row of very elegant shops located in the 200 block of the old Santa Fe Trail. While the owners of these exclusive boutiques pride themselves on their upscale styles, there is a great deal of evidence that the structure that, today houses these expensive shops, was once used by the school as chicken coops.

In addition to the stories about the chickens that once occupied these quarters, it is also said that there are permanent residents who, from time to time, make themselves known to those among the living.

There is a printing shop occupying one of these historic buildings. Many nights, members of the staff who worked late heard the sound of women's laughter and the sound of someone walking when no one could be seen.

Topping this, however, are the antics that took place in the Three Sisters Boutique, a clothing store along this row of haunted buildings. Though these buildings many have once housed chickens, it was also once the Old Opportunity School Building. However, today, this particular section of this historic old structure now houses a modern Western-wear shop.

The Boutique is owned by two women who had high hopes for their business in the tourist mecca that is Santa Fe. The first night when they counted their receipts, they came out with ten dollars too much. No matter how hard they tried, they were unable to account for the extra ten dollars. However, to their amazement, for the week, each evening they found that there was ten dollars too much in the register. No explanation has ever been found.

THE GHOSTS

Those who had lived in the area said that Sister George, a member of the Sisters of Loretto Order, known for her unselfish assistance to those of need in the community was responsible for the extra money that appeared in the register each night. She was always helping out those in the community and she had spent many years teaching in the old building.

Many said that after she died in the early 1970's her spirit started manifesting in the old Opportunity School building, where she had spent many years. The old school was purchased by Best Western Corporation and turned into upscale shops. The company spared no expense to make the old building comfortable quarters for the shop owners.

However, several tenants complained of hearing footsteps when no one was around, and of noticing strange electrical problems such as lights going on and off for no reason. There are also some shop owners who have reported than an extra ten-dollar bill regularly appears in their cash registers. Today, most of the ghostly activity seems to be cantered around the Three Sisters Boutique. The clothing shop was named for Sister George and two other nuns who ran the original school.

CAMACHO HOUSE
507 Apodaca Hill Street
Santa Fe, New Mexico

The Camacho House is old, but no one is sure exactly how old it might be. Not a lot of detailed information is known of its history, except that during the 1920s it is known that this house was used as a brothel and a gambling hall.

The old house also has a reputation of being very haunted by a number of spirits. There have been stories of a mischievous presence that likes to grab ankles and trip people who walk through the house.

Patricia Camacho was one tenant in this house that reported that she has seen the impression of an invisible person in the comforter on her bed and has heard the voices of a group of people in conversation coming from the empty basement of the house. These unearthly voices have also been heard by visitors to the house.

CHURCH OF SAN MIGUEL POR BARRIO ANALCO
Old Santa Fe Trail
Santa Fe, New Mexico

The city of Santa Fe was founded in 1610, and El San Miguel (St. Michael's) Mission Church was built between 1610 and 1628. Foundations of the first church remain observable under the sanctuary of the present structure. Archaeological investigations beneath these foundations reveal evidence of Native American occupation of the site as early and 1300 A.D. In 1680, during the pueblo rebellion, the church vigas in the ceiling were burned, and in 1692 De Vargas ordered the church rebuilt. In 1710 the church was reconstructed and a sacristy was added to its south side in 1714. Repairs to the structure were made between 1798 and 1805 and again in 1830. In 1853 Archbishop Lamy installed the altar stone[12].

In 1859 the church served as the chapel for the newly arrived Christian Brothers who took over control of St. Michael's School. In 1881 the Christian Brothers purchased the church, a recently completed school building, an adobe building and the land upon which they were situated from the Archdiocese of Santa Fe. Over the years repairs were affected to the roof, walls and floor. In 1955 archaeological investigations were made, the altar reredos and artwork were restored.

Since its creation, San Miguel has been used as a chapel and shrine to St. Michael, a military chapel, an oratory for the Christian Brothers, a school chapel and a barrio church. Today, in addition to being an historical treasure, cultural heritage and tourist attraction, it still serves as a shrine to St. Michael and a chapel where Mass is celebrated weekly.

---

[12] http://www.cbnosf.org/Old%20Church.htm

This particular story concerns not a ghost, per se, but rather the story of a miracle that has defied explanation to this day. It was actually the old bell at this church was the source of a miracle that took place in the mid-1800's.

According to local legend, a blind man attended the church at noontime every day. His fervent prayers for the return of his sight are said to have caused the bell to ring with no one pulling the rope. To the shock of not only the man but also the rest of the parish, it was said that during the time that the bell was ringing loudly, the man regained his sight. He was later able to accurately describe statues and icons inside the church that he had never seen, but to his sorrow, he became blind again as soon as the ringing of the bell stopped.

Catholic Church officials were initially puzzled, but finally described the miracle as a visitation of the Holy Ghost. The bell that caused the miracle was cast in Spain in 1356 and placed within this church. In 1872, the bell of the miracle fell from the old spire. It was left where it landed and is currently on display on the church grounds.

THE DEVIL HOUSE
934 Lopez Street
Santa Fe, New Mexico

There was once a young man whose name was reported as Michael. According to the story, he was engaged in devil worship in this house and eventually got more than he was bargaining for. It was reported that Michael joined a gang of Satanist from Cerrillos and was soon overcome by evil. He performed rituals in his bedroom and once sacrificed a dog there. Then one evening, two figures, like "huge, winged birds or bats" appeared in his room and beat him unconscious. When he was released from the hospital, Michael tried to quit the group, but never succeeded.

In September 1988, the twenty-three-year-old committed suicide by slitting his throat. Prospective tenants inspecting the house reported feeling uneasy there, and a few felt they were being slapped by an invisible hand. A priest blessed the house, and current residents have reported no problems.

LUGUNA PUEBLO MISSION
Santa Fe. New Mexico

In this old mission, it is reported that the coffin of a murdered priest that was buried beneath the floor of the mission keeps popping up through the church floor. Father Juan Padilla was murdered by Indians in 1733 and was buried beneath the floor at the Isleta Pueblo Church.

With the priest buried parishioner thought the Holy Man would rest in peace. However, to their shock and amazement, his coffin, hollowed out of a cottonwood tree, rose out of the earth in front of the altar. It rose again twenty years later, and again in 1889. Each time the coffin threatened to leave the grave, it was returned to lie peacefully for a decade or so. Finally, on Christmas Eve 1914, it poked through the floor again. This time it was decided that something had to be done to permanently end this issue. So it was reported to the Bishop who immediately organized an investigation.

In fact, there were two investigations conducted by the Bishop of Santa Fe, but no conclusion was reached as to the nature of the phenomenon.

PERA BUILDING
1120 Paseo de Peralta
Santa Fe, New Mexico

In April of 2001, New Mexico's Governor, Gary Johnson authorized the General Services Department to purchase the Public Employees Retirement Association (PERA) Building as part of a new office building in the West Capitol Complex[13]. Many locals consider the Public Employees Retirement Association (PERA) building to be haunted.

Some will not go near it because both the building and the parking lot were built on the site of an old Spanish-Indian graveyard. In fact, two levels of the five-floor building were constructed below ground in the middle of the graveyard. Unseen hands are said to reach out and trip people on stairs, and unexplained cries and moans echo through the halls. Once the ghost of a tall, thin, woman appeared in a third floor corridor. At least one janitor quit because of the ghostly activity.

Another ghost has been seen by a number of people in the parking lot adjoining the building. According to all

---

[13] Norman, Michael and Beth Scott, <u>Haunted Heritage</u>, TOR, New York. 2002.

reports, the spirit of a small lady in a black dress with a mantilla pulled tightly about her head had been seen moving quickly across the parking lot. She looks so real that a number of people who have met her speak to her, though she never acknowledges the friendly greetings.

It seems that the lady's son was a student at the old St. Michael's College in Santa Fe. St. Michael's was a boarding school with students from many distant and isolated New Mexican towns.

While at the school, the lady's son contracted the dreaded smallpox and died. Not wanting to alarm the citizens of Santa Fe with the thought of a possible smallpox epidemic, City authorities buried the young boy very quickly and in an unmarked grave in the cemetery upon which the PERA Building is now located.

The boy's mother was long in learning of his death due to the isolated location of her village. She came to Santa Fe as soon as she could, but the boy's body had long been buried and City authorities refused to tell her the exact location of his grave. She was heart broken at the death of her only child and refused to return to her home without his remains. She eventually died of a broken heart, but even today, many report that her shadow is seen as she still searches for the remains of her son.

VILLAGRA BUILDING
408 Galisteo Street
Santa Fe, New Mexico

There is another building in the Capitol Complex that is reputed to be haunted. As the first building constructed with New Deal money in New Mexico in 1934 this building was designated as the Public Welfare Building. For many years it played an important role as the headquarters for state and federal relief programs during the New Deal.

Architecturally, the Villagra Building represents the maturation of John Gaw Meem's Territorial Revival work, the signature style of Santa Fe's state government buildings. The original 1934 section, along with an addition that was added in 1953 was built of poured concrete frame finished with cream-colored stucco walls, brick coping, pedimented window and door surrounds and classically inspired columns across the front entry.

In September 2001, the Historic Preservation Division (HPD) learned that Property Control Division (PCD) was planning to demolish the historic Villagra Building on Galisteo Street, as part of their Capitol Complex Master plan, and build in its place a brand-new facility to house government offices. Their reason for the demolition was their belief that the building was no longer suitable for re-occupancy without substantial work, after its tenant of 30 years, the state Game and Fish Department decided to vacate the building in early 2001.

HPD staff quickly acted to facilitate an Emergency State Register Listing for the structure, to temporarily protect it from its demise, while trying to negotiate possible alternatives with PCD and its architectural consultants for the project. As a result of the listing on October 5, 2001, PCD and HPD entered into an agreement to save the majority of the original 1934 Public Welfare Building, while permitting the demolition of the entire 1953 addition and a portion of the northwest wing of the original structure.

THE GHOSTS

What was not widely known and was certainly not mentioned nor considered in any of the high level negotiations over the fate of this historic old building was that it is haunted.

The employees of the Department of Game and Fish, the primary tenant in this old building for many years, reported that they had often seen an old woman wearing a gown from the late 1700s era walking down the hallway.

Even more unusual, witnesses said that the old woman always had a small dog perched on her shoulder.

It was also reported that whenever someone met her, the old woman would beckon to them to follow her. But as soon as she invited someone to follow her, it is said, the old woman, and her dog, would vanish.

Inquiries about this story will result in some saying that the old woman whose spirit is seen in the building was a witch who was hung in the 1700s. The place where she was hung was located where the Villagra Building now stands. Of course, others swear that there was an early cemetery located where the building now sits and the old woman was one of those buried in the cemetery. These people say that the building of the structure disturbed the old woman's rest and now she comes back to try and chase away those who disturbed her.

CHAPTER THREE
TAOS, NEW MEXICO

The area around what is now known as Taos is a mysterious land of towering mountains and broad mesas. It is thought to have been continuously inhabited for approximately 6,000 years. During prehistoric times, nomadic hunter-gatherers roamed the valley. The ancestors of present-day Pueblo Indians, the nomads, eventually adopted a sedentary lifestyle, becoming the first farmers of the region.

Taos Pueblo, thought to be the oldest continuously inhabited structure---from 800-1,000 years--- evolved into a trading center by the 13th century. The "trade fairs" of that time drew members of the Apache, Navajo, Kiowa and Comanche tribes, and caravans from Chihuahua, Mexico.

Taos Valley changed dramatically with the arrival of the Spanish in the 16th century. When their search for gold yielded only the glint of straw in adobe structures, the New World conquerors began to colonize the valley. Attempts to dominate the Indians and convert them to Christianity, and the inevitable intermarriage, resulted in rebellion. In the Revolt of 1680, Pueblo Indians rose against their Spanish masters and drove them out of the Rio Grande Valley. The Spanish would not reconquer the region for 12 years. Despite the hostility between Spanish and Indian, they had to join forces against marauding tribes from the north and west in an uneasy interdependence.

Yet another newcomer emerged in the 18th century with the arrival of French and American traders. Taos, no more than a tiny mountain village, was transformed into a bustling trade center as wagon trains, frontier scouts and Mountain Men gathered.

Rapid-fire change continued. Following New Mexico's entry into the United States as an official territory in 1847 came another Indian revolt. Territorial Governor Charles Bent and 20 others were killed in a bloody massacre.

The once geographically isolated village became more accessible when the Atchison, Topeka and the Santa Fe Railroad reached Santa Fe. The era of American's love affair with the West had begun. As tales of the region's beauty spread, tourists, writers and artists from the east discovered Northern New Mexico's uniqueness. Some settled permanently.

In 1898, two artists with a broken wagon wheel ushered in the period that would lead to Taos' reputation as a world-famous art colony. That tradition continues, as does the legacy of the primary three cultures of Taos: the Indian, the Spanish and the Anglo.

GOVERNOR BENT HOUSE & MUSEUM
117 Bent Street
Taos, New Mexico

Charles Bent was a highly respected, much loved figure of the Old West. He was a trader and owner of a number of wagon trains on the Santa Fe Trail. He owned trading posts in Santa Fe and Taos and had many dealings with early mountain men that opened up the western frontier. He provided them with supplies and bought their furs and buffalo hides. He, his brother William, and Ceran St. Vrain built Bent's Fort in Colorado, famous throughout the West as a trading center for the Indians and early mountain men[14].

According to the writings of his daughter, Governor Bent was killed In January 19, 1847 about six o'clock in the morning. The family was in bed when the Mexicans and Indians came to the house breaking the doors and

---

[14] http://www.laplaza.org/art/museums_bent.php3

windows while some of them scaled the walls of the house to begin tearing off the roof. With little choice in the matter, the family got out of bed and Governor Bent decided to speak to them.

His wife was afraid for his life and urged him to jump on one of those horses that he had in the corral and go somewhere until the danger was over. Governor Bent replied that it would not do for a Governor to run away and leave his family in danger, if they wanted to kill him, they could kill him here with my family. Without another word, he stepped out onto the porch to ask the mob what they wanted.

The ringleader of the mob responded that they had come for his head, as they did not want any gringos to be in charge over them. Governor Bent asked what he had done to wrong them as he had worked hard to help the people of Taos and the surrounding area. The ringleader replied that he had done nothing to hurt them, but that he had to die so that no gringos would be placed over them. It seemed to be a matter of principle rather than any animosity toward the Governor.

Before Governor Bent could say anything else, some members of the mob fired arrows and guns at the Governor standing on his own porch. Though he was wounded, Governor Bent managed to get back inside his home and lock the door.

Mrs. Carson and Mrs. Boggs, and a female Indian slave had dug a hole through the adobe wall to the next house; so between the three women they helped the wounded man get to where they had dug out the wall.

Though he was seriously wounded, the Governor insisted that his children go through the gaping hole in the wall first, then Mrs. Carson and then Mrs. Boggs. He wanted his wife to go next, but she told him, you go first, as she did not think they wanted to kill her but rather him.

He finally gave in and went first, but when he was going through the narrow hole, one of the arrows that had hit him and lodged in his head scraped against the wall and hurt him terribly. In frustration, he pulled the arrow out and threw it on the floor.

As his wife was going through, an Indian burst into the room and forced his way through the hole. The Indian came through almost at the same time as Mrs. Brent and was going to shot her, but the Indian Slave girl interfered, jumping in front of the Governor's wife. She was killed instead. Enraged at accidentally killing the Indian girl, their attacker then struck Mrs. Brent on the back with the butt of his gun.

The Governor and his family moved into a little room, where he sat and began to write. Suddenly the mob burst into the room where they commenced to attack the governor once again. This time, they killed and then stripped him of his clothing. When the Governor was dead, the mob wanted to kill the family, but cooler heads prevailed and the rest of the family was spared.

The American response was somewhat slow in coming to Taos as there had been violence in many places in New Mexico. American forces arrived in Taos on February 3, 1847, which was about fifteen days after Governor Bent was murdered. On February 4, 1847, they began a roundup of the mob and fighting broke out. According to records, soldiers killed about 250 Indians and Mexicans in the Pueblo, and hung 6 Mexicans in the middle of the Plaza that were said to be the ringleaders of the Governor's murder. There were an additional sixteen Indians hung elsewhere, in town.

At the same time that the Governor was murdered, rioters also killed Sheriff Luis Estaven Lee, Cornelio Vigil, Mrs. Brent's Uncle, Provost Judge Lawyer Lea, Pablo Jaramillo, Mrs. Brent's brother and Narcizo Beaublen. In Arroyo Hondo they killed Turley the owner of the Distillery and seven men more that were working there.

THE GHOSTS

It was violent emotions that led to the Native American uprising that resulted in the murder of Governor Brent and it is said that violent emotions can lead to hauntings. So it should not be a surprise that among the spirits that are said to haunt the Brent House are those of the men who killed the Governor. They were caught and hung not too far from the scene of their crime and as a result, many believe that their ghosts still haunt his house. Their dim outlines have been seen moving about the building and their angry voices have been heard, very late at night, by staff members.

KIT CARSON HOUSE MUSEUM
113 Kit Carson Road
Taos, New Mexico

The Kit Carson Home and Museum is a complex of buildings which includes a portion of the original four room home of Kit Carson and his wife Josefa, an 1855, three-room structure known as the Romero House, and two, 1952 structures that house the museum's retail shop and additional exhibition space. Carson arrived in Taos in 1826, at the age of fifteen; Taos was to be his base of operation and home until just before he died in 1868. Carson became a trapper and mountain man and traveled extensively through out the West.

Built in 1825 with 30-inch adobe walls and traditional territorial architecture, the home's 12 rooms are today furnished as they may have been during Carson's days. The Kit Carson Home and Museum was originally opened to the public in 1952. Since that time nearly a million people have been through the Museum this has taken a toll on structures that were never intended to be more than single family homes!

Kit Carson came to Taos in 1825. He died in this house in 1868 at the age of fifty-nine.

THE GHOSTS

A number of museum employees and patrons have detected the ghost of Kit Carson in his former home. The friendly ghost of Kit Carson has been detected in the part of the museum that was his former home. The original three-room house in which Carson lived was eventually expanded to accommodate his children. Though a rough and tumble frontiersman, those staff and visitors who have seen Carson's ghost say that Carson's spirit is a very domesticated ghost and is very kind to women and children.

LAS PALOMAS DE TAOS ADOBE
240 Morado Lane
Taos, New Mexico

This historic adobe house located in the northern part of Taos was the private residence of New York socialite and heiress Mabel Dodge and her husband Tony Luhan. Mabel Dodge came to the Hispanic, Pueblo and artist community of Taos in 1916. She came to the Southwest seeking "change". Here she met the man she was married to for over 40 years, Tony Luhan, a full-blooded Taos Pueblo Indian.

Mabel was "the most common denominator that society, literature, art and radical revolutionaries ever found in New York and Europe." This claim was made by a Chicago newspaper reporter in the 1920's, of Mabel Dodge Luhan, a woman who attracted leading intellectual and literary figures to her circle for over four decades. Mabel was mistress of a grand salon, an American Madame de Stael. She was also a leading symbol of the New Woman, self determined and in control of her destiny. Luhan found her final and best-loved home in Taos. Here she married a Taos Pueblo man, Tony Luhan, and set out to establish Taos as the birthplace of a newfound Eden. She brought writers like D.H. Lawrence and Willa Cather, painters like Georgia O'Keeffe and John Marin, and activists like John Collier to help her celebrate and preserve it[15].

    Mabel and her husband, Tony started construction of the "Big House" in the 1920's, enlarging the original 160 year-old home to its present size. The 22-room house is sequestered behind an adobe wall whose gates are ancient altar pieces. Huge cottonwood, beech and elm trees shade the residence and the flagstone placita. In traditional Spanish Colonial style, a long portal crosses the house, opening to the living room, bedrooms and the log cabin studio. All main rooms have ceilings of viga and lattias construction, arched Pueblo-styled doorways, hand-carved doors, Pueblo fireplaces and dark hardwood floors. Credit for gathering many of the era's creative luminaries in Taos goes, however, to Mabel Dodge Luhan, a New York heiress, socialite, and counterculture activist. Tony Luhan, her fourth husband - to whom she remained married for more than 40 years - was an illiterate, full-blooded Taos Pueblo Indian.

    Celebrated artists, writers, and thinkers of the day flocked to Mabel and Tony Luhan's home, and some of them later made their own homes in northern New Mexico,

---

[15] http://www.mabeldodgeluhan.com/history.html

including D.H. Lawrence, Andrew Dasburg, Georgia O'Keeffe, and Leon Gaspard. Ansel Adams, Mary Austin, Robinson Jeffers, Laura Gilpin, Jean Toomer and many others were housed, fed, and nurtured in the Luhan's "Big House."

After the death of the Luhans, there have been a number of subsequent owners, which include Dennis Hopper (Easy Rider, Blue Velvet) and Las Palomas (a center for global studies which occupied the home until August of 1996). It is now the Mabel Dodge Luhan Lodging and Conference Center.

THE GHOSTS

Though Mabel was a world traveler and extremely well read and Tony Luhan was said to be illiterate, the two had a marriage in which both were apparently extremely happy. They also loved their home since both are known to haunt it.

The ghosts of Mabel Dodge Luhan and her husband Tony have been seen moving through a wall in the hall outside the bathroom and their laughing apparitions have also been observed floating in another room.

Former residents have blamed Mabel's presence for moving statues and furniture in the house. The privileged matriarch lived in the house for forty-four years, until her death in 1963.

It is said that the Rainbow Room in the old adobe home sits over a location that was used by Indians for various rituals over the years. When the original fireplace in the Rainbow Room was replaced, it seemingly disturbed on of the spirits. This spirit was said to be an Indian girl named Manuelita has been seen a number of times hovering around the fireplace. She is said to have died of natural causes in this very room many years ago.

THE GARDEN RESTAURANT & BAKERY
127 Historic Taos Plaza
Taos, New Mexico

The very popular Garden Restaurant and Bakery began in the historic Taos building at 127 Historic Taos Plaza around 1987. Prior to becoming a fashionable restaurant and bakery, this old building had been occupied by an indoor flea market and even earlier it had been a large grocery store.

It was shortly after the purchase of the building and prior to the opening of the restaurant that the owner discovered an ancient Native American skeleton hidden away in a dark corner of the basement. A few years after this gruesome discovery, the restaurant changed hands and the new owners had a priest come bless the bones. An archeologist also examined them, finding that the bones were those of a Native American female. When notified of this fact about the bones, the owners decided to give the skeleton the name of Snowflake. They also had the bones buried properly. After the burial, most people put the skeleton out of their mind and got down to the serious matter of running the business. However, the spirit of the skeleton had not forgotten them.

THE GHOSTS

The management of the restaurant has heard various stories of strange noises and other unusual events happening to the staff, however, the bakers who spend most of their time in the basement where the skeleton was found have experienced these events on a first hand basis.

There is a story that one of the bakers would always make Snowflake, as the ghost is called, her own loaf of bread and hide it on a high shelf so that no one would take it. After a day or so, when the baker would check, the loaf would always be gone. There has never been any doubt in the baker's mind that the ghost takes the offered loaf of bread.

The bakers always come to work in the very early hours of the morning so that the baked goods are ready for the business day. As they work, many times they will hear footsteps in the restaurant above them. However, when they check, the building is always found to be empty.

Due to the heat given of by the large ovens, the temperature in the basement is always very hot. However, sometimes, the bakers will feel as if someone else is there with them and blasts of cold air will fill the basement, cooling them down. They have also found that if they speak of the ghost or call her name, they will be immediately hit with a blast of bone chilling cold air.

One morning, the bakers were working hard when they suddenly heard footsteps above them in the restaurant and the sound of something loud and metal falling on the floor. Then they heard something being drug across the restaurant floor. Thinking that a burglar had broken into the business, the bakers came up the stairs and searched the building. They found no one, nor did they find anything that had fallen or that was out of place.

Others have talked of pots and pans being thrown across the room or sliding across the floor. Perhaps Snowflake just wants some company and feels that she had to get everyone's attention. After all, she spent a long time in the dark corner of that basement and no one paid her any attention at all.

THE HISTORIC TAOS INN
125 Paseo Del Pueblo Norte
Taos, New Mexico

Since 1936, The Historic Taos Inn has welcomed famous folks like Greta Garbo, D. H. Lawrence, and Pawnee Bill. More recently, celebrities like Robert Redford and Jessica Lange have been spotted sipping margaritas in the lobby.

What is today known as the Historic Taos Inn is actually made up of several adobe houses, all of which date from the 1800s. These adobes surrounded a small plaza that had been converted into the Inn's lobby. As was customary in many such enclaves, there was a community well was located in the center of the plaza. In its place today, there is a fountain surrounded by vertical vigas, two-and-a-half stories to a stained glass cupola.

What might be referred to as the beginning of the Taos Inn dates to the 1890's, when Dr. Thomas Paul (Doc) Martin came to Taos as the county's first, and only, physician. Liking the looks of the area, he bought the largest of the houses that is now Doc Martin's Restaurant.

Doc was a rugged individualist, but was dearly beloved because of his deep concern for his fellow man. Covering the county to treat his patients meant hitching up a team of horses—and later his tin lizzie—to travel for miles through mud and snow to set bones, break fevers and deliver babies.

Doc's wife, Helen, was noteworthy in her own right. A gifted batik artist, she was also the sister-in-law of artist Bert Phillips, one of the "Taos Founders." It was in the Martins' dining room in 1912 that Phillips and Ernest Blumenschein founded the Taos Society of Artists. The Martins later purchased additional buildings surrounding the plaza, renting them to writers and artists.

When the only hotel in Taos burned the same year that Doc died, Helen saw an opportunity and entered the hospitality business. She bought the Tarleton house, which was the last remaining property on the plaza and is now the site of the Adobe Bar. With the aid of Doc's former patients, she enclosed the plaza and what became known as The Hotel Martin opened in 1936.

Through the years, the Hotel Martin was the hub of Taos' social, intellectual and artistic activity. Later owners renamed it the Taos Inn, added the popular neon thunderbird sign (Taos' oldest) and the carved reception desk. In 1982, the Inn was placed on the National and State Registers of Historic Places[16].

GHOSTS

Of course, another interesting feature of the Historic Taos Inn is the fact that it seems to be haunted. The owner of another of the homes around that little plaza was Arthur Rochford Manby who is still making his presence known today. In fact, he seems to have a noticeable impact on the operation of the Inn as the kitchen of Doc Martin's Restaurant shares a wall with what was Manby's home. The end result of this close proximity to the kitchen are reports that there is a lot of ghostly phenomena that occurs in the Doc Martin Restaurant kitchen.

There have been reports of pots, pans and other kitchen appliances flying across the room to crash to the floor with a horrendous din. There have been other reports of lights flashing on and off, doors swinging open and closed without anyone near them as well as cold spots and breezes springing up out of nowhere.

Ghostly figures are also seen in the Adobe Bar late in the evening and solitary members of the Staff who are in

---

[16] For more information see http://www.taosinn.com.

the lobby late at night report hearing voices calling out their names.

A figure believed by many to be the ghost of Arthur Manby[17] has been seen in both the restaurant as well as the kitchen. He is always said to be wearing a hall brown hat and a leather jacket that is best described as faded and worn which does match many of the descriptions of Manby's favorite attire.

It is interesting to note that he does not limit his wandering to just the kitchen and the restaurant area. There have been reports that he has also been seen in the early hours of the morning in room 109. It may be of some note that Room 109 of the Inn also shares a common wall with the kitchen of Doc Martin's Restaurant. The staff has also reported that this room seems to also be colder than the rest of the Inn.

Guests who have stayed in Room 102 have reported the strong scent of roses in the air. This may be because both Arthur Manby and Helen Martin enjoyed raising roses.

---

[17] Arthur Manby is also well known because his was one of the most notorious unsolved murders in Taos. He had a reputation as a swindler and the master of the Ponzi scheme. He was also said to be the ringleader of a secret society that terrorized the region. His murder was never solved, though it was believed to be some of his closest associates that killed him. His home was what are now the Stabled Gallery and the Caffe Renato.)

In Room 106 the figure of a tall woman has been seen. The interesting thing is that when she leaves the room, she seems to do it though the mirror, which is left hanging askew after her exit. This does raise some interesting questions, as there have long been legends about mirrors being the entrance to other dimensions.

In Room 206 the original fireplace was adorned with painted figures. Many guests who were assigned that room would refuse to spend the night, mentioning that they felt that they should not be there. Once the room was repainted and the figures covered up with a cost of paint, guests reported that there were no longer any issues. The room seemed pleasant and inviting.

HACIENDA DEL SOL
109 Mabel Dodge Lane
Taos, New Mexico

Our next haunted location is the well-known Hacienda Del Sol. Built in 1804, the historic building has been home to a number of historic figures to include Mabel Dodge Luhan and her husband Tony.

A number of people spoken to that had stayed or visited this establishment spoke highly of it and recommended spending a night or two there. Though it is a very comfortable bed and breakfast, it does have some unusual aspects.

One story is that several guests reported that when they put their room key in the lock, someone inside would push it back out, even though the room was supposed to be empty.

The Inn does sit on a plot of land just outside the Taos Pueblo land. Tony Luhan was a member of the Taos Pueblo and there are those who swear that inside the room that had been Mabel's it was possible to sometimes hear a drum beating though it could not be heard in any other room in the building.

Another guest reported seeing man sitting beside the fireplace in her room. When she asked him what he wanted, his response was that he wanted certain Indian artifacts displayed on the walls of the room to be removed. She later identified a picture of Tony Luhan as the man that had been in her room.

THE ALLEY CANTINA
121 Teresina Lane
Taos, New Mexico

One of the best known spots in Taos to take a few minutes and enjoy your favorite alcoholic beverage and a nice mal is the Alley Cantina. The building itself is over 400 years old, but the really unusual events that have happened here started about 20 years ago when the owners commissioned some renovation. Many have commented o the fact that ghosts do not like change.

Some of the reports include items being moved from one place to another within the building when no one was around the move them. On another instance there were some candle sat up in the bar to be lit at night. The first morning after they had been put in place, when the owners came in to get ready for the workday, all of the candles were lit.

Finally, there have been stories about women who have gone to the bathroom feeling like they are being touched.

CHAPTER FOUR
FARMINGTON, NEW MEXICO

The history of the Farmington area dates back over 2,000 years when Anasazi lived in "pit houses" throughout the region. They later built pueblo structures from the native sandstone rock as can be seen at Aztec and Salmon ruins, as well as many other archeological sites in the surrounding countryside.

After the Anasazi's mysterious disappearance about 1500, the area was inhabited by the Navajo, Jicarilla Apache and the Utes into the present time. Native Americans called the area "Totah," which translates as "where three river meet," the La Plata, Animas and San Juan.

The Spanish passed through the region in the late 1700s and eventually settled in the eastern part of San Juan County in the early 1800s. It wasn't until the mid 1870s that pioneers from Animas City, Colorado began permanent settlement.

Originally called "Junction City" because of its location near the convergence of the 3 rivers, the town began to blossom into a flourishing farm and ranch economy and was incorporated in 1901. The name was later changed to Farming Town and finally, the "w" was dropped, shortening the name to Farmington.

Farmington's other historical claim to fame is that for 3 consecutive days in March of 1950, half the town's citizens reported seeing hundreds of "flying saucers" zooming through the skies between 11 am and noon.

LIONS WILDERNESS PARK
Farmington, New Mexico

Lions Wilderness Park is located outside of Farmington, New Mexico in San Juan County. There have been a number of stories about some strange sightings of a person who has been taking things from visitors to the park. This entity also has been known to make some strange and eerie noises in an attempt to scare visitors away from the park.

People who have camped in the park overnight report that they sometimes can hear the sounds of footsteps approaching them only to hear the footsteps stop very close to their campsite. Then they feel a hand touch them. However, when they turn on their lights, they report that there is no one there and no footprints to show that anyone had been there other than themselves.

Others say that very late at night they have heard screaming followed by laughs so scary that it makes their hair stand on end.

It should also be noted that there have been many reports of Sasquatch sightings in the general area. In fact, that part of the state seems to be an area suited to these shy creatures.

CHAPTER FIVE
CHAMA, NEW MEXICO

FOSTER'S HOTEL RESTAURANT AND SALOON
393 S. Terrace Avenue
Chama, New Mexico 87520

The building housing Foster's Hotel Restaurant and Saloon dates from the 1881 and is the oldest commercial structure in Chama. This historic old building has had quite an interesting history. As if the provable history is not enough, there are also a number of stories about the building being haunted.

According to one story, in the late 1800s there was a hotly contested election to fill a vacancy for a judge. To everyone's surprise the election was won by a woman, which horrified a number of the men in town. The night of her election was also the night she died of poisoning, apparently on the premises of the Foster Hotel Restaurant and Saloon. Her body was discovered the next morning, though the case was never solved.

A number of witnesses have reported hearing the sounds of a woman chocking and gasping for air. Perhaps this is the judge reliving her last moments on this earth. Several cold spots, often associated with hauntings have been found within the building. From one of the rooms the sounds of a young girl crying can be heard which may be associated with the death of a young girl of illness in the hotel.

On the second floor of this historic old building a dark shadow of a man is sometimes seen in Room 21and the sounds of someone walking about in cowboy boots can be heard echoing in the hallway. Guests that have stayed in Room 25 have reported finding both hot and cold spots. Additionally, there is a story that there is an antique desk chair in the room that if moved, will return to its original location on its own.

CHAPTER SIX
ESPANOLA, NEW MEXICO

ESPANOLA POLICE STATION
Santa Clara Peak Road
Espanola, New Mexico

You would think that if there was any place that was safe and secure it would be a police station, but this is not true. In Espanola, New Mexico is it the Espanola Police Station that is haunted and the locks and alarms are no barrier to this spirit.

One boring evening, those officers on night duty at the station watched their security cameras in total shock as an unidentified man walked through a gated area that was locked and protected by a sophisticated alarm system. The figure did not trigger the alarm and when several officers rushed to the area, though just seconds before the figure had been seen strolling about, there was no one there. It is reported that periodically, this figure is seen coming and going without setting off any of the alarms.

I did hear a story, but never saw any proof, that the original owner of the land upon which the police station was built was taken from its owner by the city under eminent domain. The aggrieved owner cursed the city until his dying day. Perhaps he has come back to check out the state of his former property – sort of a ghostly eminent domain, if you will.

CHAPTER SEVEN
CLOVIS, NEW MEXICO

The known history of the area now known as Clovis begins approximately 12,000 years ago with the Llano culture of the Paleo-Indians who hunted the huge mammoth and other animals. Archeological findings in the Blackwater Draw near the Curry-Roosevelt county line have traced man from the Llano culture (more commonly called "Clovis Man") through the Archaic group of the period 2500 to 500 B.C. From here, there is a gap until about 1200 A.D. when an early Pueblo group appeared. From the 1200's through the advent of white men, Plains Indians and buffalo roamed over what is now known as Curry County.

The cowmen were the first permanent white settlers in the area. They chose the semi-shallow draws which were watered by a few springs to dig their dugouts, later erecting rock homes and barns, letting their longhorn cattle drift over the open range.

In 1906, the Santa Fe Railroad chose this area to locate their "Eastern terminal" of the Belen cutoff. The site was surveyed, and the new town was quickly established. The naming of the town was no small task.

Although many felt it should have a Spanish name, there was no Spanish background to the area. The story goes that a railroad official's daughter, who had been studying French history, suggested the town be named after an ancient Christian King of the Frankish Empire. Finally, the Santa Fe Railway designated the name "Clovis" after this ancient King (Clovis I), who founded the empire, and was King of the Salian Frankish Empire, from 461 to 511 A.D.

In 1929 an airfield was developed west of Clovis for T.A.T. train-plane travel across the United States. The airfield became Clovis Army Air Field in 1942, where B-17, B-14 and B-29 bomber crews trained. The field was deactivated after World War II, but reactivated in 1951, and in 1957, was renamed Cannon Air Force Base, which has since become one of the major jet fighter training sites for U.S. Air Force. With the establishment of Cannon Air Force Base, Clovis stepped into a diversified economy that spurred growth of our modern colleges, healthcare facilities, and businesses.

Deep well irrigation beginning in the early 1950's turned the southeast third of the county into one of the most productive areas in New Mexico. Curry County grows more wheat and sorghum than any other county in the state.

Land use of the other two-thirds of the county can roughly be equally divided between dry- land farming and grassland. The grassland and wheat pasturing in the area supports the oldest industry in the county, that of raising livestock. Recently large Holstein dairies have come into the agricultural scene, and what is being billed as the largest cheese plant in the country is currently under construction.

Culture may not be the first thing that comes to mind when talking about Clovis, but it does have its share. "Clovis Music," with its small, world-famous recording studio, made history in 1957 when Norman Petty recorded and made the first hits for Buddy Holly, Roy Orbison, Waylon Jennings and the Fireballs. Today, music history continues to be made by stars such as LeAnn Rimes.

NORMAN PETTY RECORDING STUDIOS
1313 West 7th Street
Clovis, New Mexico

Figure 4: Sign for the Norman Petty Recording Studios.

Of course, everyone has heard that New Mexico is the place where the UFOs came to visit in 1947. But strange happenings have ranged well beyond Roswell, New Mexico.

Ten years later, in 1957, Buddy Holly recorded his hit song, Peggy Sue, at the Norman Petty Studios in Clovis, New Mexico, first located in an abandoned Texaco station on 7th Street and later re-situated in the old Mesa Theater.

A musician who made sounds recordings there has reported that on several occasions tapes would come up blank after a recording session, there would be absolutely nothing on them. The musicians would have to re-record the whole sequence.

Billy Stull, who became the owner after Norman Petty had passed away, swore "that Norm's spirit watches over the studio, and helps out on occasion." In other words, the ghost of Petty hangs around to make sure the musicians get it right, erasing bad tracks. There have been a number of unusual stories to come out of this well known studio.

This first story came from an internet site that is dedicated to ghosts. It is called the Ghost of the 7th Street Studio. I don't even know the name of the author, but I called some people in Clovis who assured me that the story was true.

The Ghost of the 7th Street Studio[18]

It's been almost ten years since I last set foot in Norman Petty Studios. It's been almost nine since I last performed for money. Well, unless you count the donkey show, then it's ... er ... was that out loud?

What I'm trying to say is, it's been a long time. I think I remember the history of Norman Petty's original 7th Street Studio, but memory may falter. Sue me.

---

[18] http://www.globalprovince.com/letters/10-6-04.htm

The studio itself was originally a gas station. A Texaco, I think. The gas station moved to a busier street and the property came up for sale. Norman bought it and proceeded to turn it into a studio. The front of the building became the studio proper: What used to be the sales area was converted into the foyer and the engineering booth, and what had once been part of the garage and the office was opened up and became the performance area. Unlike the Mesa Theater studio where we recorded -- with the separate booths for each instrument as well as a vocal booth -- the 7th Street Studio was wide open. Everyone played together.

On occasion, Norman actually had to move the Crickets' drummer out into the foyer. Apparently, he was so skin-happy that his drumming was bleeding onto all the other tracks. He was, therefore, excommunicated.

One of the major renovations Norman did to the studio, however, and what seemed to make recording there a most pleasurable experience, was the addition of a kitchen and sleeping quarters off the back of the studio. To get there, you had to squeeze through a long narrow hallway. (I am skinny and my shoulders only had a few inches breathing room when I walked through.) The hallway spilled out into the kitchen, which in turn led to the beds. (When I went on the tour, they still had the original two sets of trundle beds: Just enough space for the four musicians.)

Well, time went on. The world lost Buddy in February 1959 to a famous plane crash. Norman went on to do work with The Fireballs. He bought the old Mesa Theater in Clovis and turned it into his dream studio. The old 7th Street Studio became a museum.

Shortly following Norman's death in 1984, a journalist from England called Billy Stull (our producer and then head of the studio). Apparently, Buddy Holly was experiencing a huge rebirth in England. Would it, then, be possible to come take a tour of the old studio for an article?

Billy didn't see why not. When the journalist arrived in Clovis, Billy greeted him and proceeded to give him a VIP tour of the old studio. Afterwards, the journalist asked if it would be okay to sleep there that night.

Billy was concerned about this. He'd never been asked to grant such privilege before. After discussing it with Vi Petty, Norman's widow, it was decided that he could stay, but that Billy would have to lock him in the building -- you know, security. The journalist was very pleased.

The next morning, Billy headed straight for the old studio. He made a point to inspect everything on his way through the studio back to the bedroom, where the journalist was surely still sleeping. Nothing seemed out of place and no equipment appeared to be missing.

He squeezed through the narrow hallway and into the kitchen. The kitchen light was still on and as he moved closer to the bedroom he noticed that the lights were still on back there, too. When he stepped into the room, he found the journalist sitting up in one of the beds, back firmly against the wall, eyes wide open, skin white as a sheet, forehead dripping sweat.

Initially, Billy feared the man was having some sort of seizure. He rushed quickly to his side and took his face in his hands. "Are you okay??"

The journalist grabbed tightly onto Billy. "Just let me outta here!" he demanded.

Billy quickly led him out to the parking lot. After a chance to calm down, the journalist explained:

"About half an hour after you left, I heard the front door of the studio open and close. I was working on the outline for this article there on the bed. I kept waiting for you to appear, but when you did not, I went to check. The door was still locked.

"I didn't think much of it at first, so I went back to writing. Half an hour later, it opened and closed again. I set my notebook down and went to check right away. Still nothing, still locked. That time, I left the lights on in the studio. I was suddenly paranoid.

"I went to my bag and found your business card. It has your home number on it and I wanted to call you. The phones in this building don't work."

Billy shook his head. "We've never felt a need to reconnect them."

The journalist continued: "I wasn't able to get too much work done after the second incident. The third time it happened, though, I jumped and ran in. Nothing. I came back here and decided I would put on some music -- I brought my own stereo, just in case. I turned it up so that I wouldn't be able to hear the door if it opened again.

"But then the first song on the tape ended. In the silence following, I could hear other music. At first I thought it was coming from outside, and I jumped up to try and flag down whoever it might be to let me out.

"That's when I realized it was coming from inside the studio. At first, I was relieved thinking that you were here. But once I started to make my way back there, I noticed there were no lights on, even though I had left them on earlier.

"About halfway down that awful hallway, I could clearly hear the song 'Heartbeat'. But the studio was dark and I couldn't see anyone or anything. I called out, hoping to get your attention, still thinking it might be you.

"That's when the music stopped. And I could hear movement in the studio, footsteps. I flipped on the light again. There was no one else in the room.

"Then the music started again, louder. I ran to the window of the booth to see who was in there. The booth was empty. I turned and began to head out of the room. Just as I was about to step into the hallway, the lights went out and the music stopped.

"I kept moving. About halfway down the hallway, I could hear someone ... something walking in the hallway behind me. I looked back. There was no one there. I ran back to the bedroom. Only a moment later, I heard the door open and close again."

The British journalist wasn't the only one to encounter strange happenings at the old 7th Street Studio. Both Billy and Vi (among others) had heard things off and on over the years, but never anything quite as sensational as what the journalist recounted.

With a Little Help from My Friends[19]

Way back when, back before I met Ari, I was a rock star. Or at least I was pretending to be a rock star. I lived and breathed music. I played guitar for a band called The Rudiments in Albuquerque. We started as a high school garage band and eventually worked our way into three separate demo sessions at Norman Petty Studios in Clovis.

During our third session, we had been working on one song for well over four hours. Sheepishly, I admit that it had been me who was holding things up. It was a solo and for some reason there was a half-step I just kept flying right over, landing on a sharp instead of a flat note. I seem to remember we recorded that stupid line at least 20 times. Everyone else had already laid down their tracks: Jeff (our bassist) was videotaping footage for the rockumentary we were never destined to make; Stacy (our keyboardist and singer) was at ease beside Billy, our producer and engineer; Shannon (our drummer) was twirling drumsticks in the lounge. And I was still in the freakin' booth. At about midnight, we tried one more time. I still missed the half-step, but I recovered quickly. It was barely noticeable.

We rejoiced. Rather perturbed, I dropped my guitar and left the booth to hear the playback. Stacy gave me a

---

[19] Ibid

sympathetic pat on the shoulder as I sat down in the engineering room. The tape screeched softly out of the speakers as Billy rewound it.

Click! The end of the last chorus before the solo fired up. Billy cranked the volume and leaned back in his chair. We all waited, nervous. The chorus ended and slid right into the first measure of the solo.
Nothing.

Well, there was the underlying music that everyone else had recorded earlier, but no solo. Billy leaned up to the board and began to fiddle with knobs.

Still Nothing.

He shrugged. "Sorry," he said. "Let's try it again."

"Ugh," I said. Actually, that's not what I said (I'm not going to repeat what I really said).

Back in the booth, I had to retune my guitar. When I left earlier I had carelessly let it drop. I pulled the headphones over my ears and said belligerently into the mic beside the amp, "Crank it."

The tape rolled, the end of the chorus blared in my headphones and I closed my eyes. The next thing I knew, I was flying through the solo. It was like I was on a cloud. I was so tired and I remember feeling a bit discombobulated.

Before long, the music choked off in the headphones. I set the guitar down and stood, letting the headphones rest around my neck. I looked out the window of the booth and saw all my band mates cheering. Billy was sitting at the mixing board, a huge smile on his face.

I left the room just in time to hear the playback. It was perfect, no skipped step, no lagging time -- all perfectly fluid.

A little while later as we were heading over to the old 7th Street studio (where Buddy Holly recorded), Billy told us something very interesting. A few years back, he had been working with the Everly Brothers. They had been in a situation much like ours: As hard as they tried, they just couldn't quite get that last part to work. Finally, when they had reached the point where they were ready to settle, they played it back. As was the case with us, the track was gone. They were forced to re-record. And they did. And it was perfect.

Billy went on to tell us that this very same thing had happened not only a couple of times before, but many times. In fact, he had been accused on more than one occasion of forgetting to hit the record button.

Jeff promptly pulled out his video camera. He had been filming the tape deck during my second-to-the-last take. The VU meters were highly active and the red record button for track 6 (mine) was lit. It was not a human error.

Billy's interpretation of the phenomenon is this: Norman Petty had poured his whole life into music, and even more into the studios he built. The studio where we recorded (the Mesa Theater studio) was Norman's last. It was his prize, his baby. Billy believes that Norman's spirit watches over the studio, and helps out on occasion. Considering that I've never been able to recreate that perfect half-step since that night, I tend to agree with Billy.

Ghosts have not been seen first hand here, but have been photographed. Phantoms caught on film include: a group young men who were photographed in the living quarters of the old studios (now a museum) and strange orange lights were also see in the same location. Sensitive visitors have wanted to cry for no reason.

CHAPTER EIGHT
GALLUP, NEW MEXICO

Gallup's population can be traced back to 2500 BC with the settlement of the Anasazi in Canyon de Chelly. As the Anasazi population rose, so did trading in the area. By the time the Spanish Conquistadors arrived in 1540, a highly sophisticated Native American culture was thriving.

The actual city of Gallup traces its origins to the railroads and trading post entrepreneurs of the late 19th century. In 1880, while the Atchison, Topeka and Santa Fe Railroad was pushing its way slowly westward, a paymaster named David Gallup established a small company headquarters along the projected right-of-way. Rail workers soon began "going to Gallup" to collect their pay, and when the tracks were finally laid through the area in 1881, the new settlement was formally named after the paymaster.

For its first half century, the economy of the emerging town was largely supported by plentiful coal mining in the region. In fact, Gallup was for a time called "Carbon City." The town's first inhabitants were those European, Asian, Mexican and westward-seeking

American workers who sought employment in the mines, as well as building the rails.

Today, Gallup serves as a major Native American trading center. The 17.5 million acre Navajo nation is home to 210,000 people and covers parts of Arizona, southern Utah and New Mexico north and west of Gallup. The Navajo capital, Window Rock, is 28 miles northwest of the city, just inside the Arizona border. There is a Navajo Museum at Window Rock worth visiting.

OLD HOUSE ON AZTEC
Gallup, New Mexico

There is an old house on Aztec that has long been said to be haunted. It seems that this old house was once the home of a little boy named Billy. Many people have reportedly heard the sounds of Billy still romping and playing even though he died long, long ago.

You see, young Billy met his unfortunate death while quietly playing in his room, a sanctuary where he felt completely safe from the dangers of the world. Now it seems this little boy who died so young is to live eternally in the closet of the front bedroom.

Though long dead, Billy is said to be a friendly ghost, who many have said enjoys playing with the children that have lived in that room over the years.

EL RANCHO HOTEL
Gallup, NM

Formally opened December 17, 1937, The EL Rancho Hotel was built by the brother of the movie magnet, D.W. Griffith. Drawn by the many films made in the area, Ronald Reagan, Spencer Tracy, Katherine Hepburn and Kirk Douglas were among the many stars listed in the guest register. Autographed photos of the stars, Navajo Rugs & Mounted trophy animal heads adorn the magnificent two story open lobby with its circular staircase.

The El Rancho Hotel was built by Joe Massaglia in 1937 for R.E. "Griff" Griffith. Originally, Griffith came to Gallup to direct a film. He later returned to build the El Rancho Hotel. He also managed the local Chief Theater. From the 1930's to 1950's, the hotel became a temporary home for many Hollywood stars. It also became a stopping point for tourists driving on old Route 66. The hotel is now protected by the National Historic Preservation Society. This historic hotel is continually cared for by Mr. Ortega who has made it his personal hobby since its purchase.

The hotel is decorated and furnished in the Old West rustic style. It is constructed of original brick, ash tar stone, and huge wooden beams with a pitched wood shale roof. The large portico overlooks the entrance and reflects the Southern Plantation style. Entering through the solid wood doors, one views the grandeur of the lobby. The floor is brick, inlaid in a basket weave pattern, and the light fixtures are made of stamped aluminum. The stone fireplace cove is surrounded by handmade wooden staircases, that spiral to the second floor balcony. The balcony encircles the lobby and displays original photos of the hotel and many autographed pictures of the Hollywood stars. Mr. Armand Ortega has recaptured the hotel's splendor and charm of yesterday.

A large number of Hollywood's most famous movies were shot in the area such as: The Bad Man, an MGM film starring Wallace Beery & Ronald Reagan in 1940; Sundown, a Wanger film starring Gene Tierney in 1941; Desert Song, starring Dennis Morgan in 1942; Song Of The Nile, starring Maria Montez & Jon Hall in 1944; Four Faces West & Colorado Territory, both starring Joel McCrea in 1947-48; Streets Of Laredo, starring William Holden & William Bendix in 1948; Rocky Mountain, starring Errol Flynn in 1950; Big Carnival, starring Kirk

Douglas in 1950; Raton Pass, starring Dennis Morgan in 1951; New Mexico, starring Lew Ayres in 1950; Fort Defiance, starring Dane Clark in 1950; Fort Massacre, starring Joel McCrea in 1957; A Distant Trumpet, starring Troy Donahue & Suzanne Pleshette in 1963; The Hallelujah Trail, starring Burt Lancaster & Lee Remick in 1964.

THE GHOSTS
A number of guests as well as staff members have reported hearing disembodied footsteps and laughter on the upper floor of the lobby after hours.

Objects have been reported to have been moved about throughout various locations of the hotel by unseen hands. The mysterious opening and closing of doors has been reported in the bridal suite.

CHAPTER NINE
CONCLUSION

Well, all good things must come to an end and so it is with books. The stories that I have told here are not all the stories that I have collected by any means, but rather a representative sample. New Mexico as a whole is filled with stories of the strange and the unusual. In another volume I wrote about what happened when I went chasing Sasquatch in Dulce, New Mexico.

Do ghosts walk, or is it something else, some other force at work? Each of us need to decided for ourselves, though I will tell you that I have been places and seen things that can only be explained by the idea that something survives after death.

Until our next visit, enjoy.

INDEX

5

509th Bombardment group, 24

7

7th Street Studio, 133, 134, 135, 138

A

A Distant Trumpet, 147
Adobe Bar, 117, 118
Albuquerque Indian School, 69
Aliens
   Greys, 14, 15, 16
   Reptoids, 15, 18
Alley Cantina, 121
Alto Street, 77
American Committee of the Archaeological Institute of America, 81
American Indian Pueblo Council, 69
Anasazi, 123, 143
Apache, 41, 101, 123
Archdiocese of Santa Fe, 92
Archuleta Mesa, 14
Arizona, 14, 37, 38, 144
Atcheson, Topeka and the Santa Fe Railroad, 102
Atchison, Topeka and Santa Fe Railroad, 143
Atchison, Topeka and the Santa Fe Railroad, 47
Atchison, Topeka Santa Fe Railroad, 58
Ayres, Lew, 147

B

Beery, Wallace, 146
Bendix, William, 146
Bent, Charles, 102, 103
Bent's Fort, 103
Best Western Corporation, 90
Big Carnival, 146
Billy the Kid, 48
Bishop o Santa Fe, 95
Blumenschein, Ernest, 116
Brazel, Mac, 23
Bruns Army Hospital, 51, 54

C

Camacho House, 90
Camacho, Patricia, 91
Cannon Air Force Base, 130
Canyon de Chelly, 143
Carbon City, 143
Carson, Kit, 107, 108
Casa Real Health Care Center, 78
Cather, Willa, 110
Christian Brothers, 50, 51, 92
Clark, Dane, 147
Clovis Army Air Field, 130
Clovis I, 130
College of Santa Fe at Albuquerque, 53
College of the Christian Brothers of New Mexico, 51
Collier, John, 110
Colorado Territory, 146
Comanche, 101
Cooper, Milton, 12
Curry County, 129, 131

D

DARPA, 16, 21
De Varas Street, 77
Department of Game and Fish, 99
Doc Martin's Restaurant, 116, 117, 118
Dodge, Mabel, 109, 110, 111
Don Juan de Oñate, 45
Donahue, Troy, 147
Douglas, Krik, 145, 147
Dulce Papers, 15

E

El Delirio, 80
El Dilirio, 80, 83
EL Rancho Hotel, 145
Espanola Police Station, 127

F

Farming Town. See New Mexico, Farmington
Fletcher, Alice Cunningham, 81
Flynn, Errol, 146
Fort Defiance, 147
Fort Massacre, 147
Foster's Hotel Restaurant and Saloon, 125
Four Faces West, 146

G

Gallup, David, 143
Garbo, Greta, 115
Garden Restaurant and Bakery, 112
Grand, 45
Grand Canyon, 45
Grant Corner Inn, 56
Grant, John, 17, 60, 98
Griffith, D.W., 145
Griffith, R.E. "Griff", 145

H

Hacienda Del Sol, 120
Hall, Jon, 146
Harvey Houses, 58
Harvey, Fred, 58
Hayes, Rutherford B., 48
Hepburn, Katherine, 145
Historic Preservation Division, 98
Historic Taos Inn, 115, 117
Holden, William, 146
Holly, Buddy, 131, 132, 135, 141
Hotel Martin, 117
Human Genome Project, 17

I

Indian Self Determination Act in 1975, 69
Institute of American Indian Arts, 69
Isleta Pueblo Church, 95

J

Jicarrilla Apache Indian Reservation, 14
Junction City. See New Mexico, Farmington

K

King of the Salian Frankish Empire, 130
Kingdom of New Mexico", 45
Kiowa, 101
Kirtland Air Force, 43
Kit Carson Home and Museum, 107, 108

L

La Fonda, 58, 59, 60
La Posada de Santa Fe Resort & Spa, 64
La Residencia,, 60
Lancaster, Burt, 147

Lange, Jessica, 115
Lawrence Berkeley Laboratory, 17
Lawrence, D. H., 115
Lawrence, D.H., 110, 111
Legal Tender Saloon and Restaurant, 85
Lions Wilderness Park, 124
Llano culture, 129
Los Alamos National Laboratory, 17
Luhan, Tony, 109, 110, 111

M

Manby, Arthur, 118, See , See
Marcel, Jesse, 24
Marin, John, 110
Marshall, General George C., 35
Martin, Dr. Thomas Paul (Doc), 116
Massaglia, Joe, 145
McCrea, Joel, 146, 147
Mesa Theater, 132, 134, 135, 142
Mesa Verde National Park, 82
Mexico
  Palomas, 111
Montez, Maria, 146
Morgan, Dennis, 146, 147
Muroc Air Force Base, 35, 37

N

National Historic Preservation Society, 145
Navajo, 101, 123, 144
New Deal, 98
New Mexico, 11, 12, 13, 14, 15, 17, 23, 27, 28, 35, 40, 41, 42, 45, 46, 47, 48, 49, 50, 51, 56, 58, 60, 64, 68, 69, 71, 74, 76, 78, 79, 81, 85, 86, 87, 88, 90, 91, 94, 95, 96, 98, 102, 103, 106, 107, 109, 111, 112, 124, 131, 132, 144, 147
  Alamogordo, 41
  Albuquerque, 29, 53, 58, 69, 139
  Aztec, 35, 39, 40, 41, 123
  Clovis, 129, 130, 131, 132, 133, 135, 139
  Dulce, 12, 13, 14, 15, 17, 18, 19, 20, 21, 22, 23
  Farmington, 123, 124
  Gallup, 143, 144, 145
  Las Vegas, 82
  Lindrith, 14
  Los Alamos, 12, 16
  Raton, 147
  Roswell, 23, 24, 25, 26, 27, 28, 31, 32, 35, 41, 132
  Santa Fe, 45, 46, 47, 48, 49, 50, 54, 56, 58, 59, 60, 64, 66, 67, 68, 69, 71, 72, 73, 76, 78, 79, 80, 81, 85, 86, 87, 88, 89, 91, 94, 95, 96, 97, 98, 102, 103
  Taos, 57, 101, 102, 103, 104, 106, 107, 108, 109, 110, 112
  White Sands, 42
New Mexico Highlands University, 82
New Mexico Normal School, 82
New World Order, 15, 20
Night Sky Gallery, 86
Norman Petty, 131, 132, 133, 134, 139, 142
Norman Petty Studios, 132

O

O'Keeffe, Georgia, 110, 111
Oldest House, 76
Opportunity School, 89, 90

P

Pawnee Bill, 115
Peggy Sue, 132
Penitentiary of New Mexico, 71
Penitentiary of New Mexico at Santa Fe, 71

PERA Building. *See* Public Employees Retirement Association Building
Petty, Vi, 135
Pflueger General Merchandise Store and Annex Saloon, 85
Phillips, Bert, 116
Pink Garter, 85
Pleshette, Suzanne, 147
Presbyterian Medical Services, 60
Property Control Division, 98
Public Employees Retirement Association (PERA) Building, 96
Public Welfare Building, 98, 99

R

Ramey, Roger M., General, 27
Raton Pass, 147
Reagan, Ronald, 145, 146
Redford, Robert, 115
Remick, Lee, 147
Rocky Mountain, 146
Romero House, 107
Roswell Army Air Field, 23, 30

S

San Juan Pueblo, 45
Santa Fe Indian School, 68, 69
Santa Fe Railroad, 130
Santa Fe Railway, 130
Santa Fe River, 77
Santa Fe Trail, 58, 88, 103
Santa FeTrail, 50
School of American Research, 79, 81
Secret Government, 16
secret underground alien bases, 11
Sibley, Henry H., Brigadier General, 47
Sister George, 89, 90
Sisters of Charity, 87
Sisters of Loretto, 88, 89
Snowflake, 113, 114, 115
Song Of The Nile, 146

St. Michael's, 50, 51, 52, 97
St. Michael's College, 50, 51, 52, 97
St. Michael's School., 92
St. Vincent Hospital, 61, 71, 73, 87
Staab, Abraham, 64
Staab, Julia, 64, 65, 66, 67
Streets Of Laredo, 146
Stull, Billy, 133
Sundown, 146

T

Taos Inn. *See* Hotel Martin
Taos Society of Artists, 116
The Bad Man, 146
The Collaborators, 16
The College of Santa Fe, 50, 52
The Devil House, 94
The Fireballs, 135
The Glow House., 49
The Hallelujah Trail, 147
The Staab House, 64
Three Sisters Boutique, 89, 90
Tierney, Gene, 146
Tracy, Spencer, 145
Treaty of Guadalupe Hidalgo, 47

U

UFO, 13, 16, 23, 32, 35, 39, 40, 41, 42, 43
United States Air Force, 12, 42, 43
University of Albuquerque, 53

V

Villagra Building, 98, 100

W

Wallace, Lew, 48
White, Amelia Elizabeth, 79, 80
White, Horace B., 80

White, Martha, 80
White, Martha Root, 79, 80

Window Rock, 144

www.ingramcontent.com/pod-product-compliance
Lightning Source LLC
Chambersburg PA
CBHW071630080526
44588CB00010B/1352